THE
AVONDALE CHILDREN'S HOME

CELEBRATING A CENTURY OF CARING

1911 ~ 2011

Edited & Compiled by

DAVID E. BOYER

GARY E. KING

Muskingum County Children Services
Muskingum County, Ohio

Avondale Children's Home: Celebrating a Century of Caring

ISBN 978-0615559544

Book design by Aaron J. Keirns.

CONTENTS

www.muskingumkids.org

Muskingum County Children Services

Mission Statement

To lead the Muskingum County Community in the effort to protect and serve our most precious natural resource: children.

To always provide professional, appropriate, and timely services and resources which ensures intervention delivered in the best interests of children.

This story is as amazing as it is true. The words contained within are authentic and are meant to be portrayed as if they are happening in real time. Extreme diligence and care has been taken to not only identify and state the truth, but to indeed capture the emotions, geopolitical climate, and generalized feelings of the "times." Indeed, all text appearing within quotation marks comes from original sources: face-to-face interviews, conversations and recollections from individuals directly connected to Avondale, letters both personal in nature and bureaucratic, memos, affidavits, trial transcripts, case plans, contemporary newspaper accounts, and other documents and sources.

Our goal is to professionally chronicle the events associated with an outstanding human services organization that has provided continuous quality care for 100 years (1911-2011) to thousands of extremely needy children.

A Century of Caring

The Avondale Children's Home, currently known as the Avondale Youth Center, is situated on State Route 93 in the scenic rolling hills of Southeastern Ohio just outside of Zanesville, Ohio, in the quaint little town of Avondale. This region has been and is agrarian in nature with corn, wheat, and soybean being the predominate cash crops. Throughout the years, the major regional commerce has been mining, pottery, basket-making, and the shipment and transport of goods and people through road (Interstate Highways: 40, 70, and 77), rail (Baltimore and Ohio; Chesapeake and Ohio; Norfolk and Western; Erie; CSX; Norfolk and Southern), and waterway (Licking and Muskingum Rivers). It was very intentional that the City of Zanesville became the capitol of the State of Ohio from 1810 to 1812 because of the industriousness of its people, the prevalence of the regions vast resources, and the overall ease of travel.

The Muskingum County region and its citizens have long been known for their pioneer spirit, sense of adventure, and rugged individualism, which have all manifest in a great deal of civic and community pride.

The Avondale story of hope besting despair continues to be written and my fervent hope and prayer that in the year of 2111, someone will be in the position to write the history of the second 100 years of existence of this haven for literally thousands of very needy boys and girls. It was once said that the true measure of a civil society is how that society treats its children. Muskingum County can be immensely proud of all of the accomplishments, lives saved, and futures secured related to the Avondale Children's Home and the Avondale Youth Center. The Avondale Youth Center has a story and leaves a legacy that absolutely must be told. This Children's Home has in many ways served as the heart and soul of this vibrant community. The Avondale Children's Home has endured as a living testament to a community's love for and support of the most needy amongst us…abused, neglected, and abandoned children.

Through the months and years of gathering stories, procuring photos, conducting interviews, collecting data, and observing Avondale staff and children alike, it has been the blessing of a lifetime to be able to witness the many miracles that have been created due to the magic of the human heart where the ideal that success is expected and demanded and human failure is not an option.

As an individual who has humbly attempted to uplift children my entire professional career, I want to express my heartfelt gratitude to every man or woman, boy or girl, who has contributed to the completion of this book. My biggest regret of this enterprise by far is that it is not possible to personally list all contributors, each one by name, who has contributed to the enduring legacy of the Avondale Children's Home or the completion of this book.

Especially to our heavenly Father who through His love of the "little ones" has overseen this grand facility and provided much divine inspiration throughout the past century.

The history of the Avondale Youth Center is a true masterpiece of human compassion, perseverance, and hard work.

We hope and pray that you enjoy your journey.

Respectfully,

David E. Boyer, Executive Director
Muskingum County Children Services Board

ACKNOWLEDGEMENTS

Gary King, former Child Care Worker and Team Leader of the Avondale Youth Center and current Human Resource Officer and Public Information Officer at Muskingum County Children Services, has been instrumental in researching all available archives and gathering pertinent information on the Internet. Gary's enthusiasm for his role at Children Services and to this book project has been exemplary.

Aaron J. Keirns is an extremely successful writer and researcher in his own right, as evidenced by his several books chronicling local history including: *America's Forgotten Airship Disaster, Black Hand Gorge-A Journey Through Time, Statues on The Hill* and *Honoring The Veterans of Licking County, Ohio*. Without Mr. Keirns' steady advice, counsel and technical assistance this book would not have been possible.

Our gratitude goes out to all those who shared personal memories and helped to gather rare pictures and information: Bernie Hamilton, Charlie Hamilton, Don Dozer, Dean Dozer, Robert Dozer, Judi Van Meter-Jackson, Tricia Shumate-Lewis, Bill Kuhn, Edna MClain, Freda McConnell (LeMaster), Geneva Reed (Lemaster), Jackie Jones, Donna Schaefer, Cathy Musgrave, Roger & Linda Russell, Cindy Spurlock, Janet Harper, Gerry Brandt, Nate Norris, Thomas Brown, Claudia Hammack, Jill Brumage, Charlie Jones, *The Zanesville Times Recorder* and The Muskingum County Geneological Society.

A special thanks to all Avondale and Children Services Staff both past and present who without your professional passion to protect children from all forms of abuse, neglect and abandonment this miracle of Avondale would not exist.

To all of the young men and women, boys and girls who have lived at Avondale during the past 100 years. You have all faced huge family and personal challenges and your hard work and dedication in overcoming those challenges is inspiring.

To our wonderful Muskingum County community that has constantly and consistently supported Avondale and Children Services for the past century.

VOTE ON $25,000 BONDS FOR HOME

Commissioners to Put Matter Up at Coming Election

WILL OPPOSE COUNTY HOME

Chamber of Commerce Will Name Committee to Investigate

SUGGEST OTHER PLAN TO FOLLOW

Object to Children's Home for County Unless As Last Resort

URGE RECALL OF HOME PLAN

C. of C. Committee Meets With Commissioners Monday

Urging that the board of county

ISSUE WILL GO BEFORE VOTERS

Commissioners and McIntire Trustees to Confer, However

conference with the trustees of McIntire Children's Home will be by the county commissioners time this week, according to the

$30,000 BOND ISSUE ASKED

Commissioners Resolve Put Children's Home Plan to Vote

LIKELY BUILD AN ORPHANAGE

Commissioners Not Sanguine About a McIntire Contract

AUTHORIZE A BOND ISSUE OF $30,000

Commissioners to Start on Children's Home Proposition.

Avondale Will be Se—Court House News.

commissioners expect the necessary steps to

SENTIMENT NOT FOR THE ISSUE

Children's Home Proposition Will Not Carry, is Now Appears

BOND ISSUE GOES THROUGH

Much to Surprise of All, it Carries By a Small Majority

IT WAS THOUGHT IT HAD FAILED

,000 Issue Receives 7,997 Votes, More Than Half

AVONDALE TO GET CHILDREN'S HOME

Commissioners Inspect Sites There Thursday Afternoon.

TO CHOOSE ONE IN NEAR FUTU

Authentic Information

THE INFIRMARY SITE FAVORED

Commissioners Incline to It For Children's Home.

ORPHANS TO A PUBLIC SCHO

Such Is Plan of Commissioners Regarding N Orphanage.

Board Today Decide Build Home—Abo the Plans.

The board of county commi at a meeting Tuesday aft passed the necessary resolu build a county children's home action followed an inspection proposed site on the Newa yesterday afternoon. The fir toward this end will be to for bids for the preparation to come within an estimate $30,000 to $35,000. As soon plans are prepared the amoun land issue will be based upon

TRINWAY SITE FOR THE HOME

Delegation Urges Ada Home As County Orphanage.

Commissioners Will Visit Trinway to Inspect the Place.

With a view to having the coun commissioners consider the Geor Adams homestead, near Trinway, site for the new children's home delegation of more than a score Dresden and Trinway citizens, he ed by Prof. C. E. Smock, awai upon the members of the board

THE CHILDREN'S HOME

The County Commissioners Considering Its Location

Accessibility and Cash Should Be Prime Factors in the Decision

It has been a question with well-informed people as to whether Muskingum county really needed a home

cessibility, and the consequent difficulty in securing them good homes. Therefore, if these children are to

CHAPTER 1

From McIntire to Tuscarawas to Scandal

1908 ~ 1911

In the early years of what we now call professional child welfare, the orphans of all ages (from birth to emancipation) of Muskingum County were merely given a cot with very minimal personal space alongside the adult residents at the old County Infirmary, also known as the County Poorhouse. While serving as reasonable shelter from the elements and accompanied by meager meal rations, this arrangement for the care of orphaned children was far less than optimal. On May 7, 1879, on Blue Avenue near the current Zanesville High School building, ground was ceremoniously broken for the John McIntire Children's Home. John McIntire's estate called for the McIntire Fund to give all financial resources to a number of children's charities with the largest financial outlay of funds to be used "for the use and support of a free school in the town of Zanesville for the sole use of the poor children of the town." A residential home (Blue Avenue) and a school (John McIntire Academy on Fifth Street) were both built as a direct result of Mr. John McIntire's generosity.

A bitter disagreement over funding issues caused the relationship between educators, commissioners, and the John McIntire Home Staff to disintegrate in 1895 at which time the Muskingum County Commissioners contracted with Tuscarawas County authorities to house the Muskingum County Orphans in the Tuscarawas County Children's Home at Canal Dover, Ohio. This extremely inconvenient arrangement of moving children who had lost their homes and families to a distant community created further personal tragedy and expense as it cost Muskingum County 50 cents per child for placement. This contractual arrangement

Opposite Page
Newspaper clippings from *The Zanesville Signal* illustrate the public debate taking place in 1908-1909 about building a children's home and where the home should be located.

The McIntire Children's Home First opened in a house on McIntire Avenue in 1865, before the opening of the much larger site on Blue Avenue in 1880.

OFFICIALS OF THE CHILDREN'S HOME
Thomas B. Rankin   Edward Kaldenbaugh
Robert H. Nugent
George S. Evans   Moses B. Kennedy

Above
The Tuscarawas Children's Home
and its officials, c. 1908.
Photos courtesy of Kay Kuebeler.

between Muskingum County and Tuscarawas County lasted approximately fifteen (15) years.

The Tuscarawas home for boys had its problems. On February 19, 1908 a story hit national newspapers about Clara Sterling, Assistant Matron and teacher at the home. Mrs. Sterling was in charge of the home at the time while her Uncle R.H. Nugent, the Superintendent was in California. According to the February 19, 1908 edition of The New York Times, Ms. Sterling had heard from students that 10 year old Simpson Fowler had stolen a lead pencil. Ms. Sterling admitted that she wanted a confession from the boy, so she called an assembly and forced young Simpson to stick his tongue out and place it over the back of a chair. Then she allegedly pounded a tack through the young boy's tongue with a small hammer. A physician was called for Simpson's swollen tongue. The school's janitor made a complaint, and the next day she was arraigned and fined $10 by Mayor Dedenbacher. It was later reported that the incident was exaggerated by the associated press and she had only managed to scratch the boys tongue with the tack. *The Zanesville Signal* reported on February 29th, 1908 the headline, 'Accuse Woman Who Drove Tack Into a Boy's Tongue of More Brutal Cruelties'. The article describes the findings of a report by the County Board of Visitors which was prompted by the tack incident. The article states that Miss Sterling forced several boys under her charge to eat ground mustard until their mouths were burned and they became violently ill. Another boy was forced to remove his clothing, and was whipped until 'great welts stood up on his back.' Several hogs were condemned because they were afflicted with pleuro-pneumonia. These hogs were then butchered and fed to people anyway, including the board of visitors. The report states that the home is too crowded and suggests that no more children be taken from other counties. The article concludes by stating that the board wants a law enacted which would empower the state board of charities to do investigations, and examine witnesses under oath. The board stated that they lacked the power to get to the bottom of many things. However, Clara Sterling was dismissed from service on February 20th, 1908 as reported by the Chicago Daily Tribune.

DROVE TACK IN BOY'S TONGUE.

Woman Teacher Sought Confession of Lying from Pupil—Fined $10.

Special to The New York Times.

CANAL DOVER, Ohio, Feb. 18.—Accused of driving a tack through the tongue of ten-year-old Simpson Fowler, a pupil in the school of the Tuscarawas County Children's Home, Miss Clara Sterling to-night entered a plea of guilty, and was fined $10 and costs by Mayor Dedenbacher. Miss Sterling, the assistant matron, in charge in the absence of her uncle, the Superintendent, in California, admitted she used this means to seek a confession from the boy that he had stolen a lead pencil from a fellow-pupil.

"Humane Agent Jackson and I visited the school this morning to investigate," said Chief of Police Stringer to-night, before the young woman had been arraigned and fined.

"Miss Sterling admitted calling the boy before the school, compelling him to extend his tongue over a chair back, and driving a tack through it with a small hammer.

"She said she suspected him of lying in his denial that he had stolen. Several children confirmed the story."

The child's tongue was swollen to such an extent that a physician was called.

R. W. Chapman, janitor of the home, made the complaint to the Humane officer.

The New York Times
Published: February 19, 1908

Left
Newspaper clipping from *The New York Times*, February 19, 1908.

COUNTY CHARGES BROUGHT TO NEW HOME HERE TODAY

Forty-two Orphans Make Trip From Canal Dover Home.

Just 42 orphans from the Canal Dover home were brought to Zanesville Thursday morning and made the trip to their new home at Avondale over the Southeastern Interurban on a chartered car which left the station at 10 o'clock. The children are charges of Muskingum county and will be housed in the most modern manner at the new home. Three Brown children from Zanesville were also admitted Thursday.

Superintendent J. K. Bills said that the small children were in excellent spirits when they came and took to their new surroundings as a duck takes to water. The home will not be opened for visitors after the first of the coming week.

Since the $15,000 bond issued at the recent election there will be improvements made at the home which will make it one of the finest in the state. The children for the most part were glad to get back again to their home city and county. The first meal was served at noon Thursday and was out of the ordinary as a part of a regular home meal. Everything will be running smoothly in another week.

Above
Newspaper clipping from *The Zanesville Signal*, November 23, 1911 announcing the arrival of the very first children to the Avondale Children's Home.

The New Children's Home Controversy

The debate over the construction of a new home for the county's orphans began in October 1908. The Tuscarawas Home was clearly under pressure to accommodate a more manageable number of children, and to no longer accept out-of-county children. The commissioners received notice in October that Tuscarawas was no longer willing to continue their contract to house Muskingum County's poor orphans, nor had they been able to make arrangements with the Morgan, Guernsey or Licking County homes. This left them with little time to make a decision that would impact the lives of the 30-40 current orphans and the fate of those who would arise in the future. The choice was between constructing a brand new home or coming to some kind of an arrangement with the McIntire Children's Home. The commissioners believed that a new home could be established for far less than $25,000. It had also been brought to their attention that Tuscarawas was able to charge $100 per child for a year and make a profit. Muskingum County should be able to house the children at a far lower expense if they had their own home.

There was little time to make such a monumental decision. If the issue was not on next month's ballot, it would have to wait over two years for another general election. The commissioners would need to advertise at least two weeks prior to the election in order to have the issue on the ballot. The current date was October 16th with the election to be held on November 16th. Therefore,

~ 1911 ~

The first landing of an aircraft on a ship at sea takes place aboard the USS Pennsylvania in San Francisco harbor.

Ronald Reagan, the 40th US President, is born in Tampico, Illinois.

A fire kills 146 garment workers at the Triangle Shirtwaist Company factory in New York City, leading the public to call for new safety reforms.

The Supreme Court upholds an order for the dissolution of Standard Oil Company, ruling that it is a monopoly.

The New York City Public Library is dedicated.

The Computer Tabulating Recording Company, later renamed International Business Machines (IBM), is incorporated.

John McDermott becomes the first US born golfer to win the US Open Golf Tournament.

American explorer Hiram Bingham discovers Machu Picchu, the "lost city" of the Incas in the Andes Mountains of Peru.

The New York Times sends the first around-the-world telegram via commercial services; it takes about 16 minutes to circle the globe.

MUSTARD IN BOYS' MOUTHS.

Another Charge Against Miss Sterling, Who Drove Tack In Pupil's Tongue.

STEUBENVILLE, Ohio, Feb. 29.—Miss Clara Sterling, teacher at the Tuscarawas County Children's Home, who, it is alleged, drove a tack into six-year-old Sampson Fowlmis's tongue several weeks ago, is accused of other cruelties in a report of the County Board of Visitors filed with the Probate Judge to-day.

The board says Miss Sterling forced several boys under her charge to take ground mustard into their mouths until their mouths were burned, and several of them were made violently ill, and that one boy, after she had compelled him to remove his outer clothing, was whipped until there were great welts upon his back.

TEACHER ONLY THREATENED.

Miss Sterling Did Not Drive Tack Through Boy's Tongue.

CLEVELAND, O., March 2.—Investigation concerning dispatches sent out by the Associated Press from Uhrichsville, O., and Canal Dover, O., on February 18 to the effect that Miss Clara Sterling, a teacher in the Tuscarawas county home, had pleaded guilty to the charge of driving a tack through the tongue of a 7-year-old pupil, discloses the fact that such a charge was made, but on a hearing it was found that the teacher merely threatened such a punishment.

Miss Sterling was fined $10 and costs and her services dispensed with.

STEUBENVILLE, O., March 2.—A story sent from here last Friday to the effect that five children were born to Mrs. George Campbell is untrue, and the Associated Press is requested to deny it.

Top Left
Newspaper clipping from *The New York Times*, March 1, 1908.

Bottom Left
Newspaper clipping from *The Gazette Times*, March 2, 1908.

STARTLING DISCLOSURES.
Constitution Special.

Uhrichsville, O., Feb. 29.—The investigation by the Tuscarawas county board into the charges that Miss Clara Sterling an officer at the Children's Home, had driven a tack into the tongue of Sampson Fowler, an inmate, was followed by a report today that the tack was driven in so that the blood flowed from the wounds. Other testimony showed that Miss Sterling put mustard water in the children's mouths, burning them.

Above
Another newspaper article about Clara Sterling.

These newspaper articles from the *New York Times*, *Zanesville Signal*, and the *Gazette Times* which highlight the alleged harsh treatment of a teacher at the Tuscarawas County Children's Home of several children in their charge (including several placed there by Muskingum County officials). These alleged incidents and the surrounding media attention moved Muskingum County officials to determine that Muskingum County children needed to be brought back "home."

Above
Newspaper clipping with a headline that slipped by the proofreader.

the commissioners went into special session the following morning, Saturday November 17th. At this meeting the Board passed a special resolution to submit the voters a $30,000 bond issue to establish a county children's home. Their initial plan was to appropriate 30 to 40 acres of the farm occupied by the county infirmary on Newark Road. Using the infirmary land would alleviate the need to purchase new property which they were counting on to stay 'well under $25,000'. However, not everyone was in agreement with the plans of the commissioners.

The establishment of a new home sparked debate. The Chamber of Commerce publicly opposed building a new home. The Chamber argued that a children's home already existed in the county, and there should be no need for two. After all, the McIntire Home had accommodations for 100 children and was less than half full. They suggested that even if the rates were higher at McIntire than in Tuscarawas that it would be a good business practice to pay the higher rate rather than build an entirely new home. One of the McIntire trustees quoted by *the Zanesville Signal*, "Owing to the fact that we, as trustees are bound to retain such control over all inmates of the home that we can say finally whether or not a child shall stay, and owing to the fact that we could not take the county's poor children at a rate nearly as low as the present one, it is hardly possible that such an arrangement, as has been suggested, can be made". The opposition to the home also pointed out that the use of infirmary property would be in violation of the law. It was stated in the law that the two institutions (Infirmary and Children's home) shall be separate and apart. Placing the home next to the infirmary would violate this law, which would mean the county would need to purchase a site on which they could construct the home. The opposition again pointed out the added cost of acquiring such land. On October 26th, the special committee established by the Chamber met with the Commissioners for over two hours to formally announce their opposition and urge them to recall their bond issue. The following day the commissioners made an announcement that the issue would go before the voters. However, they would meet with the McIntire Trustees to see if an agreeable arrangement could be made. If they were able to come to an agreement, then the bond would not be issued.

Just a few days before the ballot *The Zanesville Signal* ran the following article:

Sentiment Not For The Issue

Children's Home Proposition
Will Not Carry, it Now Appears

"There seems to be a growing sentiment over the court against the proposed bond issue by the county commissioners for the purpose of establishing a county children's home. For this reason it is doubtful if the proposition will carry when submitted to vote at the election next Tuesday. The principal objection heard in many sources is the fact that the county does not need another children's home in view of the fact that there is already one in the county. It is pointed out that for 19 years the McIntire Home cared for the poor children of the county and they were taken away because the trustees of the home asked for more compensation for caring for them, saying that the rate then du force was under cost.

The McIntire trustees have expressed a disposition to enter into a contract with the commissioners to care for the poor children of the county at actual cost. The city's poor children are cared for under the provisions of the McIntire will. Opponents against the bond issue.

The commissioners on the other hand claim that they cannot make contracts with other county children's home and say that the McIntire Trustees are asking too much."

Clearly, the issue was not expected to pass, but it did by only 97 votes. There were 15,800 voters on November 3rd, 7,997 voted in favor. It had been generally conceded after the election that the vote had failed to carry, but over a week after Election Day a complete canvass of the vote determined that based on the total number of votes, the issue did have a majority. The passing of this bond would allow the commissioners to establish a home, however they had made a promise that they would meet with the

Above
Unidentified photo found in the Avondale archives.

Above
Newspaper ad, October, 1908.

Above
Newspaper advertisement from *The Zanesville Signal*, sponsored by The Muskingum County Local Option League, Headquarters, Room 223, Masonic Temple.

McIntire trustees to see if they could come to an agreement before they moved forward with the bond. Such a meeting never occurred. The Commissioners and members of Juvenile Court simply believed that McIntire was just too expensive to consider and an agreement would never be reached. The Commissioners continued to stress the importance of having a county home.

During the first week of December 1908 the Commissioners passed a resolution to build a new children's home. The commissioners declared that the home would be simple in all respects. It would be comfortable and spacious allowing room for up to 60 children. "It will not do to provide anything very elaborate for these children, we aim at comfort and think that children taught to support themselves by labor will make better citizens when reared in comfort rather than in any luxury", stated one of the commissioners. The building would likely be a two-story brick building with a large basement, and simple in design.

The commissioners were determined that the site should be that of the infirmary. The 40 acres of land was across Newark Road and to the west of the infirmary. It was standard practice at the time for Children's Homes to have their own schoolhouse, but the commissioner's had something else in mind. They decided to have the children attend public school rather than private believing that this would put them on even ground with the average pupil. Also, they likely couldn't afford the added expense of constructing a schoolhouse. The Locust Grove School was near the proposed site, and it was believed that a tuition arrangement could be made. Other sites were also considered. Among the more notable was the George Adams Estate, known today as Prospect Place in Trinway just outside of Dresden. The home was occupied by Mrs. William Cox. It is a brick mansion with over 20 rooms, 119 acres of farmland, and sat between the W. & L. E. and C & M. V. railroad tracks. It was reported that the Estate could be acquired for just over $20,000. Another location was The Wheeler Mansion on Marietta St. Two years prior, the State of Ohio had explored locations for a crippled children's home and Wheeler Mansion was in the running with a pricetag of $15,000. The infirmary land had also been considered but the land was considered too valuable at the time at $300 per acre, and there was no practical transportation. The old mansion was in good shape, and the rooms could easily be converted into dormitories. It was located on a city car line, and easily accessible. Part of the commissioner's argument for a county home was that of accessibility. Contracting with Tuscarawas had been cheap, however it made finding the children good homes very difficult. So, location and accessibility would need to be key in the decision.

Nearly a dozen sites had been proposed, but the commissioners still seemed determined to use the infirmary grounds. This site was the only one without pre-existing buildings on the grounds. The law which authorized the children's home came directly from a law which also specifically prohibited them from sharing space with an infirmary. Considering the opposition to the home even being built, it seems obvious that this would be a point of contention for the opposition and could easily turn into a legal battle. Still, the commissioners intention to use the infirmary grounds was all but certain, and publicly known even considering that State Secretary Shirer of The State Board of Charities opposed the site due to it's proximity to the home. The commissioners merely stated that he was unacquainted with the location. Ultimately, Secretary Shirer precluded the use of the infirmary grounds and required that a new structure be built rather than use any pre-existing home.

On May 22, 1909 it was reported that the new village Avondale would be the site for the new Children's Home. Avondale, located in Newton Township, was still in development. Advertisements for the new Avondale community began appearing at nearly the same time as the debate over the construction of the home. The Elizabeth land company advertised, "If you can make money for others, why not for yourself? Are you ambitious? Have you

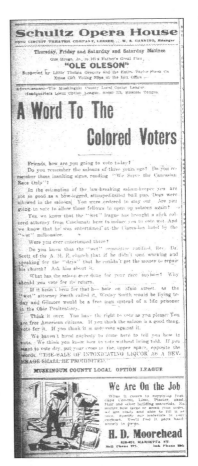

Above
Newspaper advertisement from *The Zanesville Signal*, sponsored by The Muskingum County Local Option League, Headquarters, Room 223, Masonic Temple.

Right
A typical interurban railway car much like the one that would have carried the children from Canal Dover to Avondale. Interurbans were essentially electric trolley cars that ran between many of Ohio's small towns during the early 1900s.

mastered a trade? Have you a few dollars? If so, Investigate the Opportunity of your life, AVONDALE.. 15 free factory sites, as many acres as you need. $500.00 in Gold to first factory completed. AVONDALE affords you the opportunity of a lifetime". Other ads encouraged starting a new life, and offered cash incentives for building homes. Two different sites were considered at the Avondale village. The first site was 33 acres and had been known as the Weeks property located directly across from the Avondale entrance. The second site was the Powell property which adjoined the Weeks property to the north.

Finally, as a direct result of forward thinking, thrifty and compassionate government leaders, and lay citizens, Muskingum County purchased in 1909 thirty-five (35) acres of land at the current Avondale Youth Center site. The total cost for the land was $7,572.00. This location of 4155 Roseville Road was chosen for its rural, farming potential and the interurban line which ran through Moxahala, Roseville, Zanesville, and Crooksville. Construction began immediately and after two years of construction, the Avondale Children's Home opened on November 23, 1911. On that date, forty-two(42) "little homesteaders" or "little wards" as they were referred to, arrived by Southeastern interurban on a chartered car from Canal Dover (Tuscarawas County) at the Avondale Children's Home. The children arrived around 10 am and according to superintendent Billingsley, "took to their new surroundings as a duck to water". *The Zanesville Signal* reported that, "the Children are charges of Muskingum County and will be housed in the most modern manner at the new home. Three brown children from Zanesville were admitted the same day". This was the beginning of a long legacy of children and families who would call Avondale home.

YESTERDAY'S RESULTS

Coshocton County Wet by 87...

Darke County Wet by 604

NOW—With Coshocton County and Perry County wet, an... with this county bordered on both the North and Sou... by wet territory and Licking sure to go wet on the Wes...

Can Muskingum County Afford to Be Dr...

and drained of its commercial interests from every side?

THINK THIS OVER!

Above

Newspaper advertisement from *The Zanesville Signal*, sponsored by The Muskingum County Local Option League, Headquarters, Room 223, Masonic Temple.

The temperance movement was certainly alive and well both nationally and in Zanesville in the early 1900s.

19

CHAPTER 2

The Early Years
1911 ~ 1940s

❖

The early years of Avondale have been somewhat of a mystery. For anyone who has spent much time at the home, it usually doesn't take very long to begin wondering about the past. These same brick walls have stood here and not budged for 100 years. They have seen the railway, and an era when automobiles were scarce. They have seen the farmer work a team of horses to plow the front lawn to plant crops. They would witness the final harvest 40 years later, followed by picnics, softball games and now flag football tournaments. Thousands of children and adults would pass by these bricks in years to come without giving thought to what these walls had contained. If only these bricks could tell us what they had seen.

The unfortunate reality is that there has been little time to preserve the past. As history was being made, it likely didn't seem that important. Even if it had seemed important, the day-to-day work necessary to run the home didn't allow time to preserve for posterity. Occasionally, an old-timer might show up on the steps of the building and share a story or mention a name. Often, however, these visitors are overwhelmed with emotion to be back in their childhood home, and either don't want to discuss the past or it is simply too much to handle in a brief visit. There have also been those who are willing to share what they know, but it was so long ago that they just don't remember many specifics. To make things even more difficult, all of the case records were missing for many years. They simply were not important to the modern day operations of the home. The records were stored away and not found for decades, and many have not been found at all. Perhaps

ORPHAN KIDDIES TO HEAR THE VITAPHONE

Orphan kiddies from the Avondale children's home will have a real treat Wednesday afternoon when they will be guests at the Liberty theater to hear the famous Vitaphone. The entertainment was arranged by Amrou Grotto through the courtesy of Manager Caldwell Brown. Members of the Grotto will entertain the kiddies with an automobile ride to and from the home and the full Vitaphone program and feature picture will be enjoyed by the orphans. The "kiddies" will be brought here for the 1 o'clock show.

Above
Clipping from *The Zanesville Times Signal,* November 13, 1927.

CHEVROLET CARS TAKE AVONDALE CHILDREN RIDING

The White Chevrolet Motor Co. entertained the "kiddies" Thursday when a fleet of Chevrolets were taken to the Avondale Children's home on the new Roseville road, all the youngsters and their instructresses loaded in and the entire party taken for a long ride through Zanesville and Muskingum county. There were 84 in the party not counting the chauffeurs.

Horns and other toy favors were given the children who were very enthusiastic in extending their thanks to the White Chevrolet Co.

Above
Clipping from the *The Zanesville Signal,* November 20, 1924.

ONE SCARLET FEVER CASE AT AVONDALE; FIVE OVER COUNTY

School was started Wednesday in the Avondale childrens' home following a minor epidemic of scarlet fever there. Only one case still remains at the county institution. This case has been isolated, and the other children are kept entirely away from the afflicted child.

Of the 60 children now at the county home between 45 and 50 are of school age. This necessitates having two school rooms and two teachers. One of the rooms is devoted to instruction for the younger children, while the older ones attend classes in the other. Three children of high school age attend the South Zanesville school.

There are only five other cases of scarlet fever in the county according to the records of Dr. Beatrice T. Hagen, county health commissioner. There are three cases in one family living on South Riverside Drive, one case near Adamsville and one near Frazeysburg.

Another week will see the completion of physical examination in all the county schools, Dr. Hagen says.

Above
Scarlet Fever reported at Avondale Children's Home in 1929.

ANNUAL PICNIC CANCELLED
The annual Orphan's Picnic sponsored by the Muskingum Motor club and the Cambridge Branch scheduled to be held at Moxahala park on Aug. ??, has been cancelled because of scarlet fever among the children of the Avondale home. The cancellation was made upon the advice of physicians.

Above
Clipping from the *The Zanesville Signal*, November 23, 1929.

---

most perplexing was that there did not seem to be a single photo in existence that was taken prior to the 1970's. The explanation or assumption has been that these were 'orphan' kids. The home was on the outskirts of town, because that's how the residents were viewed at the time. They were a part of our local culture that most people wanted to forget, and not see. Therefore, there would be no effort to document what happened there by picture or other means. This assumption could not be further from the truth.

As would become apparent, there has always been tremendous care about the 'kiddies' at Avondale. Chapter 1 illustrates the careful consideration of an appropriate site and the provision of the most modern facility available. Not only was the facility modern for its time, but was strategically built along the interurban railway in an area that was prime for residential and commercial development. As it turned out, both the Zanesville Times Recorder and The Zanesville Signal newspapers carried stories and updates about the home from the very beginning. The stories are numerous, but the only way to find them all and truly experience them is to go through the archives at the library page by page scanning for relevant articles in context of the era. Some of these stories were reporting on events in which the children participated, while others shared the more business/political side of things. The media often portrayed an idealized 'orphan child' image and generally shied away from the more grim realities, but it is very clear that the home was held in high regard and good news was often shared.

We would also soon discover the files and records, which were thought to have been destroyed. Several years ago it was determined that additional office space was needed. One of the upstairs rooms had served many purposes over the years such as matron quarters, houseparent bedroom, possibly the hospital room and most recently a multi-purpose storage room as it had been for many years. It was when they began updating this room into an office they discovered a large box of missing files packed into the back of a storage closet. The box contained files divided by random letters of the alphabet. It starts with 'H', followed by 'W', then 'Y' followed by 'J' with no obvious rhyme or reason. The files rarely contain any narratives about the residents, and almost never indicate when a child left or where they went. These old records did provide some clues which helped to research various topics. Stunningly, there were files dating back as early as 1912. The paper is brittle and dark with age. The handwriting is eye-catching to say

Left
It is now unthinkable to imagine the reality of medical doctors and nurses traveling to the Avondale Children's Home to perform on-site tonsil, adenoid, ear, and appendix surgeries as happened regularly and routinely at the home in the early years as evidenced by this article in *The Times Recorder* dated October 15, 1926.

the least. A calligraphic style makes the simplest words worthy of close examination. The question remained, where were the rest of the files and why were these saved? As we later discovered, most of the other files were put on microfilm and had been stored away in a small red unlabeled case. None of the files found in the box at the home were on microfilm. The only logical assumption is that the box that we found was one that -they had not, whenever they chose to store on microfilm and destroy the originals. Again, keeping the originals probably made little sense at the time with storage being an issue. If only they had known that a day would soon come when it all could have been digitized in almost identical quality and take up no physical space.

We began to seek out former residents. We found that memories were very much alive and often vivid even as far back as the late 1920's. Once people started coming forward, and sharing stories we found that there were pictures that had often been kept close to the hearts of those who lived them. This chapter attempts to shed some light on those early decades of the Avondale Children's Home, and some of those who were a part of it.

Above
Clipping from the *The Zanesville Signal*, February 20, 1928.

The First Superintendent

The first Superintendent of The Avondale Children's Home was James B. Billingsley assisted by his Wife Velma as Matron. James married Velma, daughter of George Kackley in 1897.

James Benjamin Billingsley was born at Clay Lick, Licking County, Ohio, on April 16, 1876. As a boy James Billingsley attended Fultanham High School. Enoch Billingsley, the boy's father, was injured in an accident when James was only 16 years old. Enoch was no longer able to work so James' education was cut short and he went to work to help support the family. The first job was at the South Zanesville Sewer Pipe & Brick Company

Above
James B. Billingsley, Superintendent and Miss M.M. Edwards, Receptionist.

Above
James B. Billingsley in a rest home several years before he passed away.

Below
Velma Billingsley, Head Matron and wife of James Billingsley.

earning one dollar each day. He quickly demonstrated a talent for mechanical work and was promoted to a stationary engineer. After 7 years he moved on to work for Kohler Bent Wood Works for a year and a half. He moved on to a clerkship at the Ransbottom & Randolf grocery in South Zanesville. After one year of employment he purchased the Ransbottom interest in the store which unfortunately was destroyed by fire a year later. He then returned to the Kohler plant followed quickly as a stationary engineer for 7 years at the Zanesville Tube Mill conducted by the Mark Manufacturing Company.

In the spring of 1911, James Billingsley was selected to be the Superintendent of the soon to open Children's Home. James and Velma Billingsley had many successful years at Avondale and oversaw it's operation during some of the most difficult times in our nation's history. Those who still remember the Billingsleys speak fondly of them. Sisters Freda LeMaster and Geneva Reed recalled that Mrs. Billingsley gathered the children before breakfast and they recited *The Prayer* (see page 63).

The Billingsleys are remembered as having stressed the importance of religion and good nutrition.

In February of 1926 a political movement erupted threatening Billingsley's position as superintendent. Law required that the composition of the governing board be non-partisan. At the time the board consisted of C.W. Truesdell, Clyde Reasoner (Democrats) and James Cannon and Samuel Herdman (Republicans). Commissioners Cook and Oliver made plans to appoint Democrat, former Sheriff Frick to succeed Clyde Reasoner. This was commonly believed to be a concerted attempt to name W.W. Tanner, former Superintendent of the County Workhouse, to Superintendent of the Children's Home. A shift in political power of the Children's Home governing board of Directors was at hand. It seemed an assumption that the Black-Bauerhaus political organization was determined to gain control of the Children's Home in order to place several of their members in jobs. Several weeks prior to the political shift Republican board members voted to have Billingsley's pay reduced from $150 to $100 a month in an effort to force his resignation. Efforts had been made in the past to match Matron Billingsley's pay to that of her husband. Matron Billingsley's pay was instead increased from $72 to $75 as a sad commentary on the attempt to equalize their pay. Friends and associates rallied

RE AFTER SCALP OF SUPT. BILLINGSLEY OF AVONDALE HOME

around Mr. Billingsley to fight the attempt at ousting him from his position. Supporters pointed out that Billingsley, in addition to being Superintendent, acted as Assistant Superintendent, Licensed Boiler Fireman, Electrician, and Expert Farmer and Gardener. If he was removed, then these additional positions would also need to be filled.

Ultimately, Mr. and Mrs. Billingsley retained their positions at the home where they continued to care for children until retirement in 1935. The Billingsleys' moved to a home on West Pike where they lived in retirement spending much of their time in the garden. On December 9th, 1956 Velma Billingsley passed away. Mr. Billingsley would then move to Seborn Avenue in Zanesville, followed by a four year stay at Frame Nursing Home where he would pass away on June 14th, 1965. The Billingsley's only child died in infancy. However, James and Velma raised John Gaylord, their nephew, as their own. John Gaylord later became a soldier in World War I. It is also reported that the Billingsley's had a foster son by the name of James Billingsley, who had been a resident of the Avondale Children's Home.

Above
The headlines of the *Zanesville Signal* dated February 25, 1926, illuminate rough times ahead for the Superintendent of the Avondale Children's Home.

JIM BILLINGSLEY IS RETAINED AT AVONDALE HOME

Controversy on whether or not Supt. James Billingsley would be retained at the Avondale Children's Home, was settled Monday afternoon, according to reports when the board of directors announced that the superintendent and matron of the home, who are employed under the civil service plan, would be retained.

The board of directors, with Member J. J. Frick present, met at the home Monday afternoon and elected S. C. Herdman president and C. W. Truesdell vice president. The announcement was then made that the superintendent and matron would be retained.

Above
Clipping from the *Zamesville Signal*.

APPOINTMENT WAS MADE AT MEETING HELD ON TUESDAY

Political circles were agog Wednesday following the report that Nellie N. Dye had been named a member of the Children's Home Board to succeed Samuel Herdman, deceased. The appointment was made Tuesday afternoon at a meeting of the board of county commissioners.

The appointment was specifically made to Mrs. Dye as a member of the board of trustees of the Avondale Children's Home. Members Oliver and Cook voted for the appointment while Osborn did not vote.

Various rumors followed the report of the appointment of Mrs. Dye as a member of the Children's Home Board and it was first generally believed it meant that James S. Billingsley would be removed as superintendent of the Avondale Home.

Later this report was denied and it was said that the appointment of Mrs. Dye had no political significance, whatever. Effort to confirm the report that Mrs. Dye was affiliated with the Black-Buerhaus political organization were unavailing this afternoon.

The recent appointment of a Democratic member of the board, former sheriff John J. Frick which is required under the law, was said to have meant the ousting of Billingsley as superintendent of the Avondale home.

When questioned Wednesday morning regarding any procedure that might mean a change in the superintendency of the Avondale Home or the county infirmary, Mrs. Dye was non-committal and refused to make any statements as to her future course of procedure.

Left
Clipping from the *Zanesville Signal*, November 17, 1926.

AVONDALE CHILDREN HOME SOON FREE OF ANY SCARLET FEVER

"Contagious diseases in Muskingum county are being rapidly brought under control," declared D. Hart Todd Hagen, Muskingum county health commissioner, Wednesday afternoon.

Of the many cases of scarlet which were epidemic at the Avondale children's home, only one is present and this patient is being confined in one of the older girls at the home who has had the disease and who is now recovered.

Mrs. Mary Byrne, nurse in charge of the cases of scarlet fever at the home, was dismissed Tuesday afternoon as her services are no longer required. According to Dr. Hagen, the quarantine, which has been effective at the home since the first week in April, will be lifted and the place fumigated in the near future.

Muskingum county has been fortunate in not having an epidemic of contagious diseases, according to Dr. Hagen, and the few ones that are existing in the county are under control and all quarantines will be lifted in a few days it was said Wednesday.

Avondale Memories
by Edna (Evans) McClain
Avondale Resident, October 1938 – April 1940

I had erased the memories of my stay in the Avondale Children's Home until one evening I was in the Dallas Texas Library searching for information on my ancestors. I happened to run across an entry on the 1900 Census for Zanesville. My maternal grandmother Mary Ann McGee and her sister Cora were listed as being in the John McIntire Children's Home. They had another sister but she was too young to be in the home. I started to cry and the Librarian asked me if I was all right. I told her that I couldn't understand how Grandma could have placed us in the children's home knowing that she also was in one. Memories of my experience started flooding back into my life. None of my siblings remember anything about being in the home.

Mother and Dad divorced in July of 1938 and the four of us were in the home of our maternal Grandmother and our step-grandfather, who lived on Hall Ave when we were taken to Avondale. This was some time in the middle of October. All I know was that when a big black car picked us up we were scared because we didn't know where we were going. Ruth Ann sat on my lap, Louie sat on my right, and Mary was on my left. I felt we were huddled up in the back seat. They took us to the jailhouse to visit our Dad first. I remember Dad told me he was sick, as he had eaten Harvard beets; he never ate them again.

We hadn't been there very long when one evening the older kids were celebrating Halloween by throwing kernels of corn at our dorm windows. The dorm had rows of twin size bunk beds. I slept with Ruth Ann and Mary and Louie together right next to us. I put up such a fuss when they tried to send Louie to the boy's dorm that they let us stay together for a few days. It didn't take long to settle into a routine. Dressing, bathing, and feeding my baby sister kept me busy.

My chore was dusting under the beds in the dorm with another girl. Mary was given kitchen duties when she turned 6 years old. She does not remember this and I do not remember any other of my duties but was sure I had them as everyone did their share of the work.

Shortly before Christmas 1938, Ruth Ann was gone; I don't

continued on page 28...

Left

Clipping from *The Times Recorder*, August 3, 1929, reports 3rd case of Scarlet Fever at Avondale. The accompanying ads show prices of the times.

Above

Clipping from *The Zanesville Signal*, July 9, 1948.

Above
Clipping from the *The Zanesville Signal*, November 24, **(year unknown)**.

Above
Help-wanted ad from the Zanesville Signal, March 19, 1924, advertising for a live-in, female childcare worker.

remember anything about her leaving. She was just gone. She was officially adopted on May 11, 1939. By then Louie was in the boys' dorm. Ruth Ann later stated that her adoption was not legal because her parents did not sign for them. But I read that the Board of Trustees of the County Childrens home could give their consent for adoption. The Children's Home could give consent after they found a "good home" and they could sign the papers".

I remember going to a dentist and getting some teeth filled that winter. When I was in the second grade a boy kissed me and I started to cry, the teacher asked me why I was crying and I told her. She told the boy that little girls don't like to be kissed. Also, there was another girl by the name of Edna Dunkel. She liked the boy and she tormented me during all my stay. Every one ate at long tables in the dining hall and Edna was left-handed and she sat across from me. We were taught table manners, were not allowed to talk and had to leave one hand on our lap while eating. I would pick up a fork, she did the same, I would pick up my drink she would do the same. Everything I did she did the same until I thought I couldn't stand her.

One of the happiest memories was going to Sunday school on a bus. There was a room lined with lockers and each child had a locker with a complete set of clothes and shoes. My dress was white satin, my socks had ruffles and my shoes were called Mary Janes. There was so much excitement on Sundays as we all climbed into the bus. I don't remember the church we attended but it may have been a Baptist Church

In the winter both little boys and girls played in the basement. My stepdad brought a tricycle for Louie and he would peddle that bike as we all walked around a big table singing songs. I still remember a couple of the songs we sang. We were mostly disciplined by standing in a corner outside the Matron's room. We made a game of changing corners when she wasn't watching. I know the Matron knew what we were doing even though we tried to keep quiet but she never let on that she knew. I don't ever remember seeing anyone getting a scolding or a paddling for our games. I have since learned her name was Mrs. Fred Lane. I visited the home one time and was told that Mrs. Lane had passed away before I got there and the records were stored and they could not be found. She was liked by all of us little kids.

There was a small concrete block building close to the road

and a red headed woodpecker got caught inside. The lawn was covered with dandelions and the bees loved those flowers. We didn't wear shoes in the summer but were so excited to see the woodpecker that many of us suffered with bee stings. I never forgot that spitting on a gob of mud to make a paste was good for bee stings.

In the summer, we could hear all the excitement of Moxahala Park and wish we could ride the roller coaster. One hot day a girl ran away and when they brought her back the word got around that she had BO and had to be bathed with Lifebuoy soap. We

Above
Clipping from *The Times Recorder*, February 14, 1930.

Above
Clipping from the *Times Recorder*, date unknown.

Below
Clipping from the *The Times Recorder*, June 16, 1965.

thought BO was a terrible disease.

We played outside a lot in the summer. We had a merry-go-round and swing set and played other games. I remember making mud pies and trying to get my brother to eat them. There was a tiny little yellow flower that tasted sour but we ate them. At Easter we colored pictures of bunnies and hid them outside, then hunted for them (no eggs).

We sat on the front porch and shelled butter beans in the fall. One night we had them for dinner, I just couldn't stand to eat them. Everyone had left the dining hall but I was told that I could not eat my peaches until I ate all the butter beans. I finally decided to eat them, but on the way back to the recreation room, I threw up but kept on going. Someone asked me if I threw-up in the hall and I kept saying no. They were smarter than me and knew I was telling a lie so I was put on the basement step alone with the door closed. Don't know how long but that was so scary that I always tried to tell the truth and to this day even the smell of butter beans will make me sick.

About nine or ten months after entering the home, a man and woman came and said they liked my brother and wanted to take him home with them. I was pretty unhappy so they gave me a pack

30

of Double Mint gum to pacify me. I have always felt bad because I thought I traded my brother for a pack of gum. He was officially adopted on April 16, 1940. We did not meet again until 1956 when he was told he was adopted and decided to look up his sisters. He left this world on November 23, 2010.

After he was adopted I wished I could also be adopted. The family that adopted Louie was considering me for adoption, but my paternal grandmother took Mary and me out of the home on the basis that she did not want us to be separated. This was sometime around May 1940. Grandma was in a serous accident December 1941 so we were placed in foster homes for a couple of years until Dad remarried. The only thing I remember about the first foster home (people by the name of Smith) was that we were covered with bedbug bites so we were placed in another home. I don't remember any other home, but know there were two or three others.

Christmas 1940 there were 34 girls and 38 boys in residence. We made out lists of what we wanted for Christmas. Mary received a doll baby and I received a doll high chair so we were happy. We always shared presents; the year we were with Grandma we received one pair of skates, we became very good at skating on one skate only.

I liked being in the home and looking back; I believe it was the best thing that happened to me. We were taught manners, how to share, get along with others and we had clean beds, three meals a day, and stability which we didn't have for many years after leaving. I cannot remember anything during the years I was in the 4th

and 5th grades. This time is blocked from my mind as I can only pick up graduating from the 6th grade in Columbus, Ohio. I remember this because the other girls wore white dresses but mine was pink, which was borrowed from a friend. I was so proud of that pink dress.

– by Edna (Evans) McClain

Above

Clipping from the *The Times Recorder*, September 12, **1929**. The name "Bonmetter" is apparently a misspelling of Van Meter.

Above

Clipping from the *Times Signal*, April 15, 1930. Runaways or children who go absent without leave (AWOL) have been a reality of the home since its inception due to its absence of fences, locks on the doors, security guards, and other forms of obtrusive security. However, firearms (in this case a .38 caliber revolver) are generally not a part of the equation.

Left

Edna (Evans) McClain (right), and her sister, Mary, in 1942.

Above
Clipping from *Zanesville Signal*, December 29, 1934.

"I was first placed at Avondale as a baby. Then I went to live with my aunt and returned again as a young girl. I remember doing chores in the kitchen at Avondale. I would sometimes swipe cookies and hide them down my pant leg. Then me and some of the other girls would sneak down by the road and sit and eat cookies, because we only got to eat at meal time. Sometimes we would also steal oranges and eat them at night. We would throw the orange peels out the window so the matron wouldn't find out."

Eileen Dennis, Resident, 1920-1936

The Van Meters – A Story of Tragedy and Hope

There are few stories of those who lived at Avondale in its earliest days. The case files which were missing for many years were recently discovered, but contain little anecdotal information. Events at the 'home' seldom made the news, and those who were there have long since passed. The earliest and most complete story we have is that of Charles and Morris Van Meter. A surprisingly complete file, some rare photos and extensive genealogical research from the family provide us with a unique story. The two boys were 8 and 9 respectively when they came to live at The Avondale Children's Home. The home had been in existence a brief 13 years under the care of the first Superintendent James Billingsley when they arrived on New Year's Eve 1924. One sentence in the case file is used to describe their need to be placed at Avondale, "Said minors appear to be dependent children in that the Mother is deceased and their Father is not able to furnish them a proper home". The mother had passed away, and the father wasn't able to provide for the children. This was sufficient reason to put them in the home where they would likely stay for a very long time at their young age.

The youngest child Emma Elizabeth was not sent to live at Avondale, and it is not clear what happened to her throughout this early history. It seems likely that she lived with her father on occasion, and at other times may have gone to live with different family members. As an adult, 'Aunt Cricket' as she was known, rarely spoke of her past. Although kind and generous to those in need, she was known to be a somewhat bitter person who had suffered many personal tragedies in her lifetime.

Little is known about the boys' lives before Avondale. The boys' father was Walter Everett Van Meter, occupation listed as 'Laborer but not working at present time'. Walter married his wife Mary Edna on Christmas Eve 1913 in Jackson, OH. The couple had three children; Morris Everett, 4/15/1915; Charles William 11/1/1916 and Emma Elizabeth 3/18/1918. Of course, there is no record of the life they had together other than the most basic of information. It's not possible to know what their life was like, but one can assume that they may have had the same youthful optimism and dreams for their family as any other young married couple. Sadly, the life ahead for this family would not be easy. On February 18, 1922 the children's mother, Mary Edna Morris-Van

Meter, passed away with the cause of death listed as 'dropsy'. The official cause of death was Chronic Interstitial Nephritis. Edna was only 25 years old at the time of her death. Less than two years later Walter remarried, and the two young boys, Morris and Charles would wake up in the Children's Home for the first time on the first day of 1925.

Walter Van Meter's life must have been in complete turmoil with his first wife deceased, two children living in the Avondale Home, and a second marriage now ending in separation. Employment was difficult to find, and Walter was surely haunted by the state of his family. At the time Morris and Charles went to live at the 'home', Walter was still a Zanesville resident. Walter would leave Zanesville to look for work and would eventually find it in the coal mines near Chauncey, Oh. Walter's sister Addie and her husband Clyde McNabb were living in Chauncey with their daughter Becky in the early 1930's. Becky (McNabb-Yates), has shared that life got real exciting when Uncle Walter came around. He told stories and was also a musician. Walter played the guitar, the French Harp and another instrument played between the legs that she could not recall. A note about the French Harp. "French" was often used in the US South to mean "European". Most harmonicas were actually produced in Germany, but were commonly

"Bob" Is Found Shot Along Railroad Track

"Bob," the white collie puppy of Mr. and Mrs. J. B. Billingsley at Avondale children's home, and great favorite of the kiddies there, will not be at their Christmas party this year, for "Bob" is dead. Stout little hearts that have been anxiously awaiting his return since he disappeared a few days ago, are sad today for they so wanted "Bob" to come back and share their Christmas with them.

A neighbor boy found "Bob" last night, shot cleanly through the head with a rifle bullet, lying dead along the Pennsylvania railroad tracks about a mile from the home. It is plainly evident that "Bob" was not accidentally killed. Could there not be a law against such persons?

Right
Avondale Front Field: Morris Van Meter is standing behind the wagon (see arrow).

Above
Newspaper ad from the *Zanesville Signal*, August, 1930.

called the French Harp in the South. In Ohio, a more common term would have been "mouth harp". She further recalled that Walter later married an elderly woman who was very nice. He seemed to be happy and to have found peace in his later years.

Becky remembers as a young child there was a coal mining strike in Chauncey, and Walter was a miner at the time. Walter used to tell stories about sneaking up on the young militia soldiers while they were eating, and firing shots at them to disturb their mealtime.

Gun Battles Staged; Bridge Dynamited, Fires Started

In Several Zones Rifle and Gunshot Pour Into Camp Of National Guards

"Columbus, Ohio, July 12- (AP) – Gun battles, a bridge dynamiting, a fire and a near riot marked developments today in the 3-month old Ohio mine strike. One man was killed in a gun battle at Chauncey, a New York Central Bridge near the same village was dynamited and the AHA and Michigan Railroad bridge at Albany was fired early today in what authorities said was an attempt by striking miners to intimidate workers. Almost immediately af-

ter the bridge was dynamited an undetermined number of persons began pouring rifle and shotgun fire into the national guard encampment. The guardsmen returned fire but whether anyone besides the one dead was killed, officials were unable to determine.

A near riot resulted in Belmont county when Sheriff Howard Duff and a number of deputies attempted to break up a crowd of pickets, National Guardsmen, were summoned and dispersed the crowd."

News stories about the Ohio mine strike, such as the one above, spread across the country. It was depression-era, and it wasn't easy finding steady work much less provide for a family. Events such as these show just how hard it was for many people, and why so many children were sent to children's homes not just in Ohio but across the country. The land was flooded with hobos traveling the streets and railroad tracks looking for work and ways to get through each day.

While their father spent his younger years looking for work, his two sons were growing up at Avondale. The 'Home' was much like other institutions of the time. It had a relatively small staff managing many children of different ages. Punishment was im-

Above
Newspaper ad from the *Zanesville Signal*, 1931.

GLORIOUS TIDINGS OF THE NATIVITY USHERED IN WITH PRAY'R AND SONG AT MIDNIGHT

Fewer Services Than Usual, However Mark the Advent of Christmas in Zanesville— Great Generosity Is Displayed by Local Folks for the Unfortunate of City and County

Christmas was ushered in with prayer and song at a few local churches, but the number holding midnight services was much smaller than last year. An edict by Bishop Hartley, of Columbus, caused the Catholic churches to abandon this service save in private chapels; hence, the only Catholic midnight mass was that held at the Good Samaritan chapel which was attended by the Sisters and some of the patients.

The midnight service at St. James Episcopal church was largely attended. Grace church is one of the churches which did not keep up its annual custom of holding a midnight service; however, this morning there will be special services at both Catholic and Protestant churches, and this evening a number of the Sunday schools will present programs.

Christmas is really Children's day and will be celebrated as such at the Avondale home where at 7 o'clock this morning the children, numbering 75, will be admitted to the assembly room where a stately Christmas tree, laden with gifts, will gladden their hearts. These gifts were purchased through subscriptions received at The Times Recorder office.

Christmas Day of Celebration

The McIntire Home children will have a big tree, with plenty of gifts, made possible through the contributions of friends. There will be a Santa Claus at both home's and a delicious chicken dinner will be served at the noon hour. Both homes are gaily decorated with Christmas greens and red's. There are 26 children at the McIntire home.

The sick will be remembered today at both hospitals, where a special dinner will be served with turkey as the piece de resistance. The Bethesda hospital is beautifully decorated for the occasion.

At the Good Samaritan special masses will be said in the chapel which is exquisitely decorated. The decorations extend throughout the rooms and wards.

It is no wonder that the Elks are called 'Benevolent and Protective.' This tide is ripely given. This morning the Elks will assemble at their home, South Fourth street, and at 5 o'clock they will start out laden with gifts for the unfortunate. Precisally 309 Christmas baskets will be distributed. These will contain a Christmas dinner complete, toys for the children, where there are any, clothes for the illy

clad and in some instances money. Every home an Elk visits today will be richer materially and in spirit because of the spirit of universal brotherhood which prompts these benevolent men to these acts of mercy.

The Day Nursery children have had their tree at the nursery, with gifts, and the splendid tree and treat at the Central Presbyterian church, made possible by the Kiwanians.

A delicious turkey dinner will be served today at the Helen Purcell home, with all the trimmings. This is the gift of the Central Presbyterian Brotherhood.

The inmates of the county infirmary, numbering 86, will partake of a bounteous chicken dinner today. Numerous Christmas services have been held there by various organizations and gifts of fruit and candy have been made. At the county jail, where the prisoners number 53, a well balanced meal will be served at noon, including roast veal, mashed potatoes and gravy, cold slaw and pumpkin pie. Mrs. Bradford is giving the matter her personal attention and the prisoners will want for nothing for an comfort today.

mediate and severe. The children went to school, church and spent most of their other time doing farm work and chores. Life could be hard at the Avondale Home in those early days, and being sent to live in the home usually would mean staying there till age 18. The threat of the Lancaster Industrial School loomed for those who severely misbehaved. Some children held on to a sense of hope that they would go back to live with their families. However, most were resigned to the fact that their parents were just too poor to take them back, and it was unlikely that they would be adopted. Three meals a day, clothing and a place to sleep weren't such a bad trade-off for most during those years.

On January 13, 1930 Charles, now age 13, was sent to the Bureau of Juvenile Research for an evaluation reportedly because of 'being sulky, stealing and untruthfulness'.

The following is an excerpt from the Bureau report:

"After Charles' mother died the father placed Charles and his brother* David in the Avondale Children's Home near Zanesville, OH 43701. We have no detailed authentic information concerning the offenses of these boys. Charles admitted stealing one dollar from a matron's room on each of two occasions. He said the other boys made him do it. He also admits running away from the Children's Home on about five occasions, fighting, smoking and general disobedience. He claims not to know why he did these things but insists that he is cured now and only desires one more chance to make good.

His cousin is also at the bureau at present. Her sister-in-law has been here several times to visit her. Recently she informed us that the boy's father, Walter Van Meter, married a worthless woman sometime after his wife died. The couple separated in less than a year. Mr. Van Meter then traveled around for a time but apparently settled down recently with his parents and daughter, at Mudsock, near Chauncey, Ohio.

The daughter-in-law of Charles' uncle told us further that Charles' father was working steadily as a miner, and was very eager to have his sons returned to him. We were considering the advisability of urging the placement of Charles and David with their father when the father's brother appeared at the bureau with his daughter-in-law and informed us that Walter VanMeter had just deserted his daughter again, this time hinting that he was going to Texas. The uncle felt that the reason his brother again disappeared was that he feared prosecution for having neglected his sons. We were informed that he had once served a workhouse sentence for neglecting his daughter."

*The family of the boys' mother refused to call Morris by his given name, and instead called him David.

Above
Newspaper ad, August, 1930.

Above
Circa 1948: Charles Van Meter

Opposite Page
Clipping from the *Zanesville Signal*,
April 3, 1931.

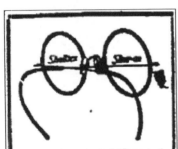

Above
Newspaper ad from the *Zanesville Signal*, 1924.

From The Bureau of Juvenile Research Report:

"Charles has told us that he was at the Children's Home continuously for five years with the exception of a trial placement one summer on a farm when he was 11 years old. He said that after hauling manure for ten days he was returned to the Children's Home. He added that if he cannot be placed with his father, he would prefer to be placed with his 'Uncle Angus' in Columbus or with some other relative. He seems to like farm work pretty well."

The Bureau case report paints a picture not unlike many of the other children in the home at the time. The days started early and ended late working the farmland and discipline was likely harsh. It is well-documented that many children in those early days were placed as a result of a deceased parent, and a surviving parent who was unable to care for them due to reasons such as financial means, alcohol abuse, imprisonment, sickness or 'insanity'.

No one knows exactly what the experience was of the two boys while in the home, but it must have been a difficult time. Since both boys were sent to The State Bureau of Juvenile Research, it is apparent that they had problems or behaviors beyond what the home was willing or able to handle at least during that time. Charles ran away from the home on at least five occasions, and on the last never returned. It is believed that he lied about his age and went straight into the Coast Guard as a 16 or 17 year old. He later retired from the Navy as a Chief Boatswain Mate after serving 30 years, and passed away in 1984 at the age of 67 survived by his wife, Lucy Dean Wham-Van Meter, a true "Southern Belle" of South Carolina, and two children, Charlene and Charles Jr.

The story of Morris is sadly one of tragedy. Morris served in the United States Army in World War II and was stationed in Wyoming between 1939 and 1940. In January of 1941, Morris wed Ernestine Humphreys. Together the couple had three children, Marlene (b. 1941), Judith Ann (b. 1944), and Verna Jean (b.1946).

As an adult, Morris was described as a caring man with strong religious faith. He was known to be witty and humorous with a love of pulling pranks. As a caring father, he often did 'without' to provide for his children. He once used cardboard to cover the holes in his worn out shoes while he saved money to buy his daughters a red "Radio Flyer" wagon. Judi remembers being quarantined in the hospital with polio as a young child. She recalls looking out

OFFICIALS PAY VISIT TO AVONDALE HOME

County Commissioners W. S. Osborne, W. R. Burckholter and Elias Kincheloe, Probate Judge John P. Baker and County Engineer George R. Evans were dinner guests Thursday at the Avondale Children's Home. They made an inspection of the home and were profuse in their praise of the services of Mr. and Mrs. J. H. Billingsley, superintendent and matron of the home.

At the present time 144 children are being taken care of at the Avondale home and the visitors made the inspection for the purpose of determining what might be needed at the home and what plans could be made to take care of any necessities.

Preventable diseases incur an economic loss of approximately $15,-000,000 annually in Virginia.

FRED LANE TO BE NAMED MEMBER OF AVONDALE BOARD

County commissioners were preparing today to appoint Fred Lane, of South Zanesville, as a member of the board of directors of Avondale children's home. He will undoubtedly be named within a few days.

Lane succeeds the late John Holloway, who served as a member of the board for more than 10 years. Two weeks prior to his death, Holloway was reappointed to serve as a member of the directorate.

In the event of Lane's appointment, Democrats will control the board for the first time in a number of years. E. B. Graham and Mrs. Kelly Weaver are present Democratic incumbents. W. L. Timmons and Henry Johnson, other members serving on the board, are Republicans.

Lane was proposed for the position by W. R. Burckholter and W. T. Osborne, Democratic members of the board of county commissioners.

Above
Clipping from *Zanesville Signal*, July 7, 1932.

Below
Clipping from *Zanesville Signal*, February 13, 1935.

LANE NAMED TO AVONDALE POST

Fred Lane and Miss Marjorie Gibson will succeed Mr. and Mrs. James B. Billingsley as superintendent and matron at Muskingum county children's home at Avondale on March 1, it was announced today by trustees of the institution.

Appointment of Lane and Miss Gibson was made at a meeting of trustees held in the office of W. L. Timmons, First National bank building, Thursday evening.

Lane, former member of the board, resigned last Tuesday, and E. M. Tincher, Republican, of South Zanesville, was named in his stead. Fo...

---

the window and seeing her father holding Marlene's hand as they both waved to her and even from a distance she felt the love of her father. Morris used to spend his lunch breaks, while working as a landscaper, playing with his daughters. He would give the young girls piggy-back rides, gallop around pretending to be a horse and entertain his young girls any way he could.

Morris would go on to work for Suburban Motor Freight as a dock worker, but was eventually laid off. His next job was for the Accurate Window Cleaning Company in Columbus, OH. It's unclear how long Morris worked as a window cleaner. It was this job that ultimately brought a tragic end to the life of Morris Van Meter.

The Columbus Evening Dispatch,
July 21 1949, front page.
WINDOW CLEANER FALLS 4 FLOORS

"A window washer was seriously hurt shortly after noon Thursday when he plunged from the fourth floor at rear of the F.G. & A. Howald Co. building, 34 N. High St, into Pearl St.

The victim was Morris Van Meter, 35, of 1048 Dennison Av, an employee of the Accurate Window Cleaning Co., 366 Clinton Heights Av.

He was taken to St. Francis Hospital by emergency squadmen suffering a broken heel, right wrist and possible back injuries.

No one saw Van Meter fall from the window but several employees of the Howald Company were attracted when they heard the thump of the man's body as it struck the pavement in the middle of Pearl St.

Police said they believed Van Meter was preparing to climb into the fourth floor window sill when he toppled to the ground. A bucket of water was still inside the building. He had not attached his safety belt to the window frame.

Mrs. Grace Kopp, 166 Kelso Rd. whose office is at the rear of the Howald store said, 'I saw him land in the alley. He didn't make a sound.'

P.H. Brodt of Grove City, another Howard employee, said he was standing on the loading platform at the rear of the store when heard Van Meter strike the pavement.

'It sounded like a roll of carpet had fallen down.' Brodt said. He said Van Meter was lying face up in the street when he turned around. Brodt said Sam W. Moffitt, 3006 Indianola Av, was also on the platform at the time."

Morris never regained consciousness after the fall and died 13 days later.

It is well documented that Matron Billingsley felt strongly about the inclusion of faith in the lives of the children at Avondale. Each day Matron Billingsley would have the Avondale children recite a bible verse for each letter of the alphabet at breakfast, and the children were taken to church each Sunday. Ernestine would later tell her daughter Judi that her father was very religious and God was an important part of his daily life. Everyday her father read bible verses to the family before going to work and went to church each Sunday. On the day of the accident, Morris was running late for work and for the first time she could remember he did not spend the time with his family reading his daily verses.

The Columbus Dispatch,

August 3rd, 1949.

FUTURE GLOOMY FOR FAMILY FOLLOWING DEATH OF FATHER

By CARL DE BLOOM

"Mrs. Ernestine Van Meter and her three small daughters, Wednesday were afraid to look into the future. A series of tragic events that was climaxed with the death of the father and husband this week has made them fearful of what life may still hold.

The family of Morris Van Meter came to Columbus from Jackson, Ohio seven years ago and life in a new town held promise of happy days to come. Mr. Van Meter found a good job with a local freight company and the couple made their home at 1048 Dennison Av.

Their third daughter was born three years ago. Their children are Marlene, 7, Judith, 5 and Verna Jean, who will be 3 on Aug. 14.

About the time the family celebrated the arrival of Verna, Mr. Van Meter was ordered to the hospital for an operation. Things returned to normal for the family but a year later trouble struck again.

Above
Newspaper ad from the *Zanesville Signal*, 1931.

41

BOY SCOUT TROOP TO BE ORGANIZED AT AVONDALE HOME

Fifteen Boys There Ready to Take Up Work; Plan Troop For Adams Mills

Scouting will be carried into the Avondale Children's home if the plans of local scout officials are put into effect. Dr. R. P. Gillespie is planning to start a troop at the home within the next month with James P. Billingsley, the home superintendent, as scoutmaster and the directors as commisioners.

Several other counties have started similar work and it has proven beneficial to the young wards in many ways as scouting aequaints them with the outdoors and interests them in a profession which they can follow after being dismissed from the institution.

About 12 or 15 wards at the home will be eligible to scout membership and with these lads as a nucleus, a patrol can be organized. The troops in other counties are smaller than this number but satisfactory results are being obtained.

After investigating the possibility of starting a troop at Adams Mills, the scout officials, Dr. Gillespie, Dr. Axline and Ralph Miller, Red Cross examiner, returned to this city last Tuesday and stated that an organization will be effected within the next month. Prof. W. H. Linn, principal of the high school, will be in charge of the troop.

Delmar Pugh, ranking active scout in this city and who is in charge of the work, will return to his home Tuesday and start the fall season of scout work in the local schools. He has been spending a two weeks' vacation with friends at Ironton.

Above

Newspaper clipping reports organization of Boy Scout troop at Avondale Childrens' Home.

This time it was a disease dreaded by all families-polio. The victim was Judith Ann. For three months Judith was in Children's Hospital.

After long months of patient care Judith recovered and now has very little effects from her illness. The family thought it had its share of troubles, but the first of this year Mr. Van Meter lost his job.

To keep the family going he took a job as a window washer. With the weekly pay check cut in half, Mrs. Van Meter went to work in the dish-washing department of a downtown restaurant.

Mrs. Van Meter, a frail woman of 33, took the job despite the fact she had been ordered to the hospital for an operation. As yet she has not had the operation but has continued to work.

Despite these setbacks the family's hopes were high. Then on July 21, Mr. Van Meter tumbled from the fourth floor of the F.G. & A. Howald building, 34 N. High St, where he was washing windows for the Accurate Window Cleaning Co.

He was taken to St. Francis Hospital and never regained consciousness before his death Tuesday. He was 34.

Completely alone, Mrs. Van Meter faces the task of paying rent, supporting three children and somehow finding a way to solve her own health problem.

Mrs. Van Meter is not bitter. She is dazed by the tragedy. A bright ray of light came into the modest Dennison Av house Wednesday when Ralph Bennett, executive secretary of the Family and Children Bureau, 337 S, High St. announced the bureau would take over the family.

He said they would investigate the situation immediately and offer whatever assistance is necessary.

Mrs. Van Meter also found a helping hand from the Columbus Police Department.

Patrolman William Allard, a police radio operator, lives at 1049 Dennison and he and Mrs. Allard have been doing what they can to help the Van Meters.

Since in Columbus, the Van Meters have not made too many acquaintances. Patrolman Allard will handle the funeral arrangements for Mrs. Van Meter and off-duty members of the department will serve as pallbearers.

Services will be held Friday at 10:30 a.m. at the Shaw-Davis Funeral home. Burial will be in Union Cemetery."

The struggles continued for the family of Morris Van Meter, but better times were ahead. The children, grandchildren, and great-grandchildren of Morris and Charles continue on with the memories and legacy of their family. In 2005, Morris' daughter Judi visited Avondale having recently discovered that it was his home as a child. For the first time, she and her family were able to see the land he had once worked, feel the brick walls which housed him, and get a better understanding of what life may have been like so long ago for their patriarch.

– Genealogical research by Marlene Van Meter-Smith, 1941-2003

Avondale Memories
by Dean Dozer
Avondale Resident, 1935 – 1947

As I recall I entered the home in 1935 and stayed there until March or April of my sophomore year in high school in 1947.

I remember several of the matrons during this time: Miss Biggs, Mrs. Miller, Mrs. Squires and the Superintendents: Fred and Louise Lane, Mr. Hutson and his wife Blanche.

I remember huddling around the radio in Miss Biggs room, listening to The Lone Ranger and Tonto, Fibber McGee and Molly, The Inner-Sanctum, Henry Aldridge and several others. I also remember listening to the fights on Saturday nights when Joe Lewis was the top fighter. Many of us were at the radio after the Japanese attack on Pearl Harbor to hear FDR give his speech saying, "This day will live in infamy."

We didn't have video games or television to take up our leisure time so we spent most of our time outdoors. We played all the sports in season: football, basketball, baseball and hockey with a crushed Pet milk can for the puck and bent tree branches for the stick. There were always enough guys so we could have competing teams. One incident that stands out while playing football was when I sewed the cardboard numerals 22 on my black turtleneck sweater. That was the number of Ohio State's all American run-

Above
Jesse Hutson, Superintendent, 1945-1949,

Above
Newspaper ad from the Zanesville Signal, 1924.

Children's Home Is Overcrowded

Institution Built for 42 Now Has 70 Inmates

The Avondale children's home is now overcrowded, James B. Billingsly, superintendent of that institution, declared Sunday night. Four children of Mrs. Pearl Kyle, of 80 Canal street, who were temporarily committed there Saturday, could not be accepted because of the crowded condition of the home.

The Kyle children were returned to their home and are now being fed and cared for by the home management, Billingsly stated. He said there are now 70 inmates of the institution, which provides for only 42 children. There are also approximately 70 other children who are in private families and are being taken care of by the Avondale management.

ning back, Les Horvath. While at the home, I was able to go to South Zanesville and play sandlot games on Sunday afternoon. As a result of my playing football in the home, I was able to play four years of varsity football in high school, two years at South Zanesville and two at Philo.

Other than sports we found many ways to stay occupied, including rolling down the hill in an automobile tire, playing marbles, potsies and ringsies, making a wire hoop and guide to roll around the grounds playing red rover. Surprisingly I don't remember anyone getting a broken wrist or arm.

We did other things, some approved and some we done unknown by management. We used to throw ears of field corn in the fireplace where we burned trash, to get parched corn. We wore a lot of coveralls and we would brand our heels with the hot metal buttons that had been placed in the fireplace. We went barefooted all summer so the bottoms of our feet were like shoe leather. It was not as painful as it sounds. We just walked on our toes for a few days.

We always had chores to perform, and each week or so a list was posted assigning jobs to each of us. Some of these jobs were cleaning the toilets, washbowls, dressing room, dormitory, setting rooms and other things that escape my memory. The job I finally got after many years was being made barn boy. Our chores were all related to farming, such as milking cows, taking care of the horses named Bob and Tom, working the fields, making the hay, shocking and thrashing wheat, hoeing and cutting corn and husking corn all day. I had a paper of Happy Jim chewing tobacco and I swallowed some of it and got very ill. That cured me of ever chewing tobacco again.

As barn boys we got to participate in helping other farmers in the community to thrash their wheat and fill their silos. We helped them and then they came to help us. It was hard work but the food was so good, all the mashed potatoes and gravy, meat, side dishes and the delicious pies. The Butlers, the Holloways and the Dodds were the ones I remember. The home also made us available to the local farmers to help with hay-making, cutting and husking corn. They paid us and fed us well. I worked and learned from some great farm managers at the home, Fred Huffman, Frank Starkey and one other whose name escapes me. They all taught us how to do many things and I remember them saying, "Don't stand around, you can always find something to do."

We were self-sustaining. We raised our own meat, we butchered hogs, had a smokehouse where we cured the meat. We had chickens for eggs and meat. We raised a big garden where we produced many vegetables. There was always a big patch of potatoes. We stored them in a bin under the laundry room, during the winter we had to de-sprout them. We made our own lye soap for laundry purposes.

We were not always little angels. We would go thru the corn field to Hammond grocery to buy BB Bats, cream filled cupcakes, pop and other goodies. It was not unusual for us to leave the premises to go swimming in Jonathan Creek. We had a ritual that we followed, that was to skip rocks across the water with the belief that the snakes would be scared away. This always preceded our swimming.

I guess all boys on the farm smoked roll-your-own cigarettes with corn silk. We also used golden rod leaves and when the yellow appeared on the paper we knew we were getting nicotine. The best smokes were when we crossed the swinging bridge over Johnathan Creek, cut thru Moxahala Park and bought Kool cigarettes at a little beer joint across the road. We were never caught doing this.

Speaking of being caught, if we messed up there were several ways we were punished. It could be an apple or willow branch across the ankles, a paddling with a paddle or a strap, or sitting on

Above
November 1943 newspaper article announcing the closing of The McIntire Children's Home. Less than a dozen children lived in the home during its final months.

Above
The McIntire Children's Home was razed to make way for the new Zanesville High School Building. The plan to build a more modern home after the war never came to fruition. Article dated, Sept. 6, 1944.

"Where do I start!? I am 88 and my sister, Freda, is 93. My brother, Kenneth, is gone but he was there also. We had special dresses to go to First Baptist Church every Sunday. All boys and girls rode together on a large city bus. This was a special thing for us. I didn't have to work, but you were considered one of the bigger kids if you did. I volunteered to wax the long hall that wen through the center of the building, about 50 to 60 feet, on my hands and knees because Mrs. Billingsly, the head Matron wanted it done. There was a large dining room with long tables with chairs. Boys sat at one side of the room and girls on the other side of the room. The young teenage girls washed the dishes. Each of us had 1 large table to wash & dry and sweep the floor under it. There were about 40 kids at each table. We all took turns for 1 week. We would try to be the first one done. Usually there were 50-60 children living there at that time. During the Great Depression there were as many as 82-84. They put beds in the hall, washrooms and setting rooms. The dormitory was packed full of beds with children sleeping two to a bed."

Geneva (LeMaster) Reed, Resident, 1928-1934

the wooden benches for a designated period of time which was the most feared.

Our school consisted of two rooms. Mrs. Lee was one of the teachers. Each morning she would read Ernie Pyle's column to us. He was a war correspondent. We were required to learn religious quotations, say the pledge to the flag and even had prayer. During the time I was there, we had an outbreak of scarlet fever and we were quarantined in the school.

We were required to go to church each Sunday. We went by bus to the Fair Oaks Baptist Church. Milt Wilson was one of my Sunday school teachers. He was a foreman in one of the factories in Zanesville. He would often relate stories as to how he found ways to demonstrate his Christian faith in the workplace.

Each year we went by bus to the Muskingum County Fair. As we got off the bus, we were given a quarter to spend, later that was raised to fifty cents. This was the only money that we received during the year. During the year we would buy items from each other with the promise, "I'll pay you back fair day".

On Sundays we would take long walks off the home ground.

Our living quarters were heated with radiators. On cold wintery days we would put our clothes on them and sometimes we would even sit on them to get warm.

I could go on and on but I'll close with a few observations. I along with my brothers and sisters missed a lot by not growing up in a normal family situation, but we all turned out to be good citizens. I will always be grateful for the strong work ethics instilled in me. I also began my faith journey while in the home. The employees at the home taught me the value of self-reliance and personal responsibilities. Their teachings also instilled in me a love of my country. I was happy that later on I was able to serve my country as a member of the U.S. Army.

– by Dean Dozer

Avondale Memories
by Robert Dozer
Avondale Resident, 1935

On one occasion when we boys came in from the hay fields, we liked to go swimming. I remember one time I went to the front office and asked the Superintendent if we could go swimming if we didn't go near the water, he groaned and said how can you swim if you don't go near the water?

At one time the older boys held boxing matches in the South corner of the apple orchard. Popeye was the one to beat (Lloyd Lanning).

Each year we were taken to the Muskingum County Fair by charter bus, and each child was given 25 cents to spend for the day.

Each and every Sunday we transported to Fair Oaks Baptist Church on Woodlawn Ave by charter bus, and our driver was named 'Shorty'.

Every year on November 11th we were driven into Zanesville to view the Veteran's Day parade, usually from the 2nd floor of the 1st National Bank building.

The older boys were the ones who worked in the fields with the farmer; we fed the stock, milked the cows, fed the chickens, gathered the eggs, slopped the hogs and watered the horses. I always heard that Avondale Children's Home was on 40 acres.

At Christmas time some of us would sneak into what was called the sewing room and watch presents being placed under the Christmas tree.

I was one who was a bedwetter, and there were many times that I had to sleep in the bath tub.

Two of the worst beatings I ever had in my life happened at Avondale. One was given by the Superintendent with a razor strap; the other one was by my school teacher.

I went through nine years of school on the grounds. When I was in the 4th grade there was a scarlet fever epidemic, I had to take the 4th grade over again. They tore the seats out of the building and put beds in.

At one time me and Bill Parr another boy ran away from the

home. Bill and I traveled to Buckeye Lake to a family member. We returned to Avondale, and then I was sent to the Bureau of Juvenile Research in Columbus, Ohio for 3 months.

During the summer the older boys were each given a section of lawn to mow with a hand push mower.

During the 2nd world war, we were not allowed to wear shoes during the summer because of the ration stamps.

During the 2nd World War, food was in short supply. At times we had to steal from the garden. Sunday evening meals we left the dining room hungry.

Going to the dining room to eat we had to line up by size and fold our arms and march to the dining room.

I heard at one time there were 50 boys and 50 girls at the home.

At Christmas time each child was allowed to ask for 3 gifts not to exceed a certain price.

We were allowed to organize a Boy Scout troop within the home, our Scoutmaster was Frank Claudy.

Twice a year we were treated with candy; Easter and Christmas. Other rare times candy would come from families.

Often times we were allowed to take long walks, sometimes to the back woods, and maybe to the swinging bridge which goes to the park.

During the wintertime when there was a lot of snow. We went sled riding behind the home to a large hill; we rode on a 10 man bobsled made of wood. It took 2 or 3 boys to pull it back up the hill.

Each summer on the 4th of July we had a huge picnic on the front lawn, and the boys and girls were all there.

At times we skated on the concrete between the home and school. Also at time we enjoyed listening to the radio in the Matron's room, this was before television. We also played games in the basement.

When the farm manager was on vacation I was asked to fill the stoker when needed.

There was a huge apple orchard right behind the home. I spent a lot of time climbing the trees and eating green apples. We called the apples green chickens. I can't recall why we called them that.

I can remember during the winter, I would set out in the field,

---

OUR CHARTERED CHILDREN'S HOME

Well, the children's home at Avondale has a charter at last, which brings to an end much ado about nothing.

Now that the home has been chartered we wonder if the children there will be any better cared for, be better clothed, better fed or be any happier. Chances are they never knew they were not living in a chartered institution and now that they are chartered, they will not care one whittle if they are or not.

Muskingum county maintains this home, has competent men and women to conduct it, and a board of good citizens to supervise it and we, who are responsible for it, don't give as much a whittle as the children do, if it is chartered or not.

This charter business is just another one of those fine sounding things that gives a lot of clerks a lot of easy money. A state inspector comes snooping around every once in a while and must find some fault with something or other to make it appear to another chairwarmer in Columbus that he has really been doing something.

One of them came down here and made a big hullabaloo about the records and said that Probate Judge Ernest Graham would have to correct the records for 11 years back. But our probate judge didn't scare worth a darn and he didn't correct the records, and it was for the little political hanger-on who stirred up all the mess, to draw in his horns

Our children's home is chartered now, whatever that means, but nobody concerned seems to care one whit if it is or not. Muskingum county erected, maintains and pays for the home and Muskingum county knows that conditions there are very good, and further Muskingum county does not care if the snoopy state inspectors like it or not. The action last week simply shows that so long as it pleases us the inspectors have simply got to be satisfied. We can now take our little ol' charter and hang it up on the string of other tin and leather medals which have been awarded us in the past.

Above
Newspaper ad from the *Zanesville Signal*, 1931.

wind blowing and snowing hard husking corn by hand sitting among the fodder.

I remember at Harvest time we would go to different farms and help other farmers during wheat harvest and silo filling time. The meals were great.

I remember I was farmed out to pick strawberries on the Mc-Farland farm on Maysville Pike. I have to say as I look back on the time I spent at the home it was the most wonderful time of my life, it was best for all 5 of my brothers and sisters.

I have to say in my eighty plus years in the time I spent at Avondale as I look back they were very fond memories.

Each school year I and all students enjoyed a movie every Wednesday in the basement of the school; educational films and a cartoon.

Each night when we were in bed certain Matrons would sit on a single bed and read a story to all of us, then lights out. Bedtime in the summer was 9:00, and in the winter it was 8:00.

When we 5 children were taken to Avondale I was quite upset with the judge, but as I grew to an adult Judge Crossland did the right thing for all of us. I learned about church, and I was taught good manners that I use to this day.

The farm horses names were Bob and Tom.

I remember the 1937 snow and ice storm when all of us boys waded up to our knees in snow going to school. The snow was that deep.

At times the health nurse would visit to give vaccinations; all children were required to have the shot. There were a lot of sore arms.

When boys needed haircuts, a barber would come to the home. Haircuts were done in the laundry room building.

Chickens were killed and cleaned in the basement under the laundry room, and also the hogs were processed there.

When eating in the dining room we were taught to eat everything that was put on our plates whether we wanted it or not. I remember one breakfast I ate the same bowl of cereal three times. I threw it up twice; the matron stood behind me and made me keep it down.

– by Robert Dozer

Avondale Memories
by Donald L. Dozer
Avondale Resident, 1937 – 1945

I was placed in Avondale Children's Home in 1937 at two years old. My older brothers, Bob and Dean, and two sisters, Shirley and Peggy were already in the home. I was told I was placed in a foster home when I was born and when my foster mother got sick and could no longer care for me she placed me in the home with my brothers and sisters. I was not aware that I had any brothers or sisters until I got older. When I arrived at the home Mr. and Mrs. Fred Lane were the superintendents. I can remember, at an early age, I was assigned chores-everything from mopping floors, cleaning the bathrooms, washing windows, hoeing weeds, picking vegetables, plucking chickens, peeling potatoes and feeding chickens.

The children's home had a school for first thru eighth grade. One year there was an outbreak of scarlet fever and we were quarantined at the school and missed having school for the whole year. My favorite teacher was a Mrs. Ashcroft, a very nice lady who encouraged us to always do our best.

The home had a large truck patch (garden) and raised all of our own vegetables, raised chickens, hogs and dairy. I remember many nights going to bed hungry and us kids would sneak down to the garden after dark and eat the different vegetables; there was no such thing as an after supper or bedtime snack.

When it was mealtime we would form a line according to height and march into the dining hall. We had to eat everything on our plate and there were no second helpings. During the summer time we would go without shoes until school started then we would get hand me down shoes.

We had several matrons at the home. My favorite matrons were Mrs. Biggs and Mrs. Adams. Mrs. Biggs reminded me so much of my Grandma Dozer. I also remember at Christmas time we were given one present. One year I remember the Moose Lodge of Zanesville had a Christmas party for all of us kids. We were taken by bus and treated to dessert and given a present.

Another time I remember the night the water tower caught fire and the fire trucks with their sirens on came to put out the fire. All of us kids ran to the windows to watch. Every Sunday morning

Above
Newspaper ad from the *Zanesville Times Recorder*, 1930.

we would all get on a bus and go to Fair Oaks Baptist Church in Zanesville. The bus ride was the highlight of the day. For entertainment we would play different marble games, roll-a-hoop with a wire handle, roll down a hill inside a rubber tire, pretend riding a horse with a stick and a piece of string or rope for the reigns, throw green apples off the end of a stick. I remember having the mumps on both sides and not being able to go to a balloon parade in downtown Zanesville with the other kids.

I also remember sneaking through a corn field and running across highway 93 to Hammonds Grocery Store and buying BB Bats (taffy on a stick) for a penny. I was lucky and never got caught. When Mr. and Mrs. Lane left the home a Mr. and Mrs. Jesse Hutson were hired as the new superintendents. Every year we would board a bus and go to the Muskingum County Fair for the day. We were given 50 cents to spend.

During my years at the home we had several head farmers, Mr. Starkey, Mr. Ayers, and a Mr. Huffman. They were in charge of the farm operation at the home.

I remember a very special person at the home by the name of Freddie McFarland. He was 17 or 18 years old and would play with us little kids and teach us how to throw and play baseball and football. Sadly, Freddie was killed while serving our country in 1943 when his ship was torpedoed in the North Atlantic.

In the summer of 1945 (10 years old) I was placed in my first of three foster homes. I remember being lined up with the other kids and was picked to go and live with a farm couple and work on their farm.

– by Donald L. Dozer

Closed---For The Duration

Pictured is the McIntire Children's Home building on Blue avenue which was closed last fall for the duration of the war for reasons of economy. At lower right is portion of iron fence surrounding tomb of John McIntire, one of the founders of Zanesville.

At the time this picture was taken but five children were enrolled at the home with accommodations for 125. The state welfare department recommended it be closed and the children, two boys and three girls placed in state-approved boarding homes in Muskingum county.

Left
Newspaper article, c. 1944.

Webers' Home Store

| Over Forty Years Of Faithful Service | Next to Court House | A Most Convenient Place to Shop In |

FOR OUR OCTOBER FALL FESTIVAL SALE
WE HAVE SECURED
A Wonderful Group of Coats

AND PRICED THEM

$49

Beautifully Furred Dress Coats models that exactly reflect the distinctive styling of much higher priced coats—in a group representative of the new winter modes. Bloused backs, straight line models that wrap in generous fashion, and models with loose panels—every coat is richly furred with large collar and cuffs of selected skins. Suede or pile fabrics of warm textures and soft finish. Immaculate tailoring.   —Fourth Floor

FOOTBALL FASHIONS

Left
Newspaper ad, October, 1926.

The Sunday Times-Signal

December 3, 1939

CHILDREN'S HOME HAPPINESS REIGNS

COUNTY PROVIDES CONTENTMENT TO BOYS AND GIRLS

By Stoughton Conover, Times Signal Staff Writer

To the average person orphans are something about which the funny papers, nursery rhymes, and sentimental holiday ditties wax alternatively hot and cold.

That same average person avidly reads his comic strip, tunes in his radio, and teaches his own children the nursery rhymes with a fine show of interest, but then proceeds to let the subject become an accentuated cipher of his daily thinking.

He might do otherwise, however, if he knew that he himself was contributing to the support of nearly a hundred boys and girls, and if he knew something of the life these youngsters led in the "homes" the county governments maintain for them by means of his contributions as a taxpayer.

That is exactly the setup Muskingum County operates for its homeless children at the Muskingum county Children's Home, located at Avondale, just seven miles south of the Zanesville City limits. It was to picture, for the unconcerned average citizen the inner workings of this institution that this writer visited. Superintendant and Mrs. J. Fred Lane at the big stone building this day and toured the entire plant.

Visitors are first received in a near office that fronts the entrance, and there they may make any arrangements or ask any questions that enter his mind. Mr. and Mrs. Lane are two ex-teachers who are in love with their work and they are more than gracious in telling the stranger about and making him see and 'feel' the operations and problems that accompany their big jobs of being mother and daddy to 72 youngsters of all sizes and ages.

The first question that usually arises is just "who" the children in the home are, and "how" they happen to be there. It is perhaps the simplest of all questions to answer.

The 34 girls and 38 boys are here because both parents are gone, because through the death of one the other cannot adequately care for the child, or because divorce or marital strife has made the home an unfit place to raise a young person.

Above
Clipping from the *Sunday Times-Signal*, December 3, 1939.

All admissions and commitments are made through the county probate judge, and youngsters may be placed in his hands by request of friends or relatives or by court order where necessary. Improper support and supervision are generally the causatives in this last case.

Some admissions are made on a temporary basis only. This happens when there is a likelihood that a parent or guardian may soon be re-established through remarriage or a betterment of his financial position. But in all others full legal guardianship is given to Mr. and Mrs. Lane, and neither the parents nor the child may exercise any control over its activities without their consent.

After a few minutes chat with this soft-spoken couple the visitor knows such consent is never withheld where it could be rightly given however. They fairly glow with enthusiasm concerning their wards, and their every effort is towards giving them as natural and normal a youth as possible.

Avondale Trustees Resign

At a meeting of the trustees of the Avondale Children's Home Wednesday afternoon Mr. and Mrs. Fred Lane, superintendent and matron of the home, tendered their resignation effective on March 1. Expressing their desire to retire from these duties, the resignations were accepted.

At the same time the four members of the board, Welcome Gillogly, Harold V. Tom, Mrs. Vashti Jones Funk and Attorney Ernest B. Graham, submitted their resignations to the county commissioners, explaining that such resignations would give the commissioners an opportunity to carry forward any program they might have in mind concerning the home.

The trustees in submitting their resignations to W. F. Herron, Elmer E. Burton and Roy Baughman said:

"Whereas it has been brought to our attention that it is your judgment as the board of county commissioners of Muskingum county that the children that are now in the Muskingum County Children's Home, and those that are to be placed there in the future can be taken care of more efficiently and economically, and to the best interests of the children by abandoning the operation of the home and placing the children in private homes.

"Now, therefore, in order that you may have an absolute free hand in the carrying out of your judgment and plans in these matters it is the unanimous opinion of the members of the board of trustees of said home that we should tender our resignations effective at once and in accordance with that opinion we hereby tender said resignations.

We take this opportunity of thanking you for your many courtesies and favors and if we can be of any service to you at any time in the future in the carrying forward of your plans the board as a unit or the members as individuals will be only too happy to serve you in any way they can.

Contacted following the resignations county commissioners said they had no comment to make at this time.

Mr. and Mrs. Lane have served the Avondale home for the past 10 years and their resignations were accepted with regret. Following release from their duties Mr. and Mrs. Lane plan to take a long rest.

Tour Begins

At this stage the actual tour of the building and grounds begins, swinging through the hall. The first stop is the boys dormitory in the north wing. It's 8 p.m., so the younger tykes are already far gone in dreamland. A swarm of blue-overall clad's are flocked about the communal study-tables, however, and these grin up as the visitor is introduced to their governess a big, motherly woman who has a room in their apartment and oversees all their work, does their mending, and tends to the little ones. Her's is a 24 hour-a-day job indeed.

Proof of this comes midway in the introductions. A tiny, night shirted little shaver with sleep laden eyes pads in from the sleeping porch, and with tugs at the voluminous governess skirts complains, "Gotta tummy ache."

When this is remedied he is led back to bed, and as he's tucked between the sheets long rows of double-decked iron cots are revealed as sleeping facilities for the "men," whose ages run all the way from 2 to 18.

Back in the living room, a long hall with a well-scuffed wooden floor and chair-banked tables, the rest of the boys are still pouring over their school lessons for the next day. There is a radio in the room, but common consent rules that it shall not be played after supper time. Their two-room school keeps them stepping, and they are proud enough of it to work hard at its assignments.

In the building's center is the dining hall. Here the boys and girls separated while in their own quarters, meet together for breakfast at 6:30 a.m., lunch at 11:00, and dinner at 4:30 O'clock.

On the south side the girls live in duplicates of the boys' quarters with a slight difference in that the facilities are a little less battered by roughhousing and games.

A really modern, comfort-laden living room in the front supplements both of these quarters, and there are the older more settled young men and women are allowed to spend their evenings in study or with books or magazines.

Every individual in the home is expected to spend a portion of his or her day at some useful work, a regulation that not only lightens the duties of the institute employees, but affords admirable practical training and self-discipline as well.

Fully Equipped Laundry

Kitchen work takes in a fully equipped laundry that weekly handles over 200 sheets, pillowcases, towels and an equal number of personal garments and one thousand and one other little domestic duties fill up this period for the girls.

The boys do their trick assisting the home's farmer tend the 8 cows, 2 horses, 20 hogs, and 250 chickens that furnish all the milk, butter, eggs, pork and towing power needed in the establishment and its 46 acres of cultivated or grass-sewn land. Corn, wheat, hay and garden-truck are raised in the summer months.

No child is kept on one job long enough to become dulled by its monotony, for all are shifted about on a regular rotation schedule that gives them a week-at-a-throw at each 10 tasks.

Work is done before going to school, just following breakfast, or immediately after the evening meal. Most of it requires not more than an hour of daily effort.

As already mentioned, the Muskingum home can boast of its own two-room grade-school manned by two township paid teachers who instruct the children in all grades from first to tenth. The older students are sent to Zanesville to attend Roosevelt junior and Lash high schools.

Medical needs are given attention in a small hospital room which is fitted for elementary surgery and isolation of contagious illness. Dr. Ray McDaniel of East Fultonham is the attending physician who is on call when needed, and the county health supervisor. Dr. Beatrice Hagen, annually conducts complete physical examinations for all **inmates** there. All children must pass a complete physical checking including a Wasserman test and all inoculations and vaccinations, before entering the home.

Organized recreation takes on many forms, but on the physical side the best known unit is the boys basketball team that plays in the Newton township school league every Friday during the season. This year they nearly ousted the eventual winners in a battle for top spot.

The girls play softball, croquet, roller skate, and work up a lather over volleyball during the warm months. Both must get their exertion in two basement playrooms during the winter.

On the social side it would take a dictionary to list their activities. Music classes are conducted by East Fultonham music

Many Applicants For Avondale Home Post

More than 20 persons are expected to file application for the position as superintendent of Avondale Children's Home as a result of the proposed resignation of James Billingsley, which probably will be submitted to the board of trustees Thursday.

The position as superintendent is under civil service and the state civil service board expected to announce date for the examination shortly. Selection of a successor to Billingsley will be made from the three applicants graded highest.

The name of Walter Burckholter, South Seventh street, present county commissioner whose term expires January 1, has been mentioned strongly in connection with outstanding applicants for the position

Above
Clipping from the *Zanesville Signal*, December 5, 1934.

Left
The word "inmates" is once again used to describe and define the child residents.

Opposite Page
Newspaper article, December 28, 1944. The Superintendent, Matron and four of the five trustees resign to allow the Muskingum County Commissioners 'absolute free hand' to close the Avondale Home.

Name Trustees For Avondale

The Muskingum county commissioners yesterday announced the appointment of new trustees for the Avondale Children's home to succeed those who recently resigned.

New trustees are: Paul Campbell, South Zanesville; Miss Dorothy Keyes, 24 Cemetery avenue; Mrs. Fred Phillips, 285 Taylor street; G. E. Wilson of Zanesville route 1, and W. O. Harper of near Roseville.

Terms of the all new appointees expire on March of the following years: Campbell, 1945; Miss Keyes, 1946; Mrs. Phillips, 1947; Wilson, 1945, and Harper, 1949.

The new trustees will meet soon to elect officers.

They replace Welcome Gillogly, Mrs. Mary Vashti Funk, Ernest Graham and Harold V. Tom, who resigned Dec. 27 after they said the commissioners displayed a "spirit of indifference" toward the management and problems of the home.

The commissioners also announced the re-appointment of Dr. E. M. Brown as physician at the county jail and at the county infirmary.

Above
Newspaper article, January 5th 1945, states that the prior trustees resigned after they said the commissioners displayed a "spirit of indifference" toward the management and problems of the home.

Party for McIntire Home Children

Children of the McIntire children's home will be entertained this evening with a hay-wagon ride and a wiener roast.

Rufus Minnick, of the West pike, will provide the transportation for the children and their friends, numbering about 40. Thtey will go to Rehl's grove on the West pike for a wiener roast, This will be followed by a ride, before returning to the home.

Miss Louise Pletcher, the matron, will accompany the children.

Above
Newspaper article dated November 3, 1942.

teacher Norman Wooley each week in the summer and a 20-piece "rhythm band" lets the boys work out noisily with drums, tambourines, whistles, castanet sticks, and a varied assortment of general instruments. A glee club gives soul treatment to the girls.

Every Sunday afternoon two women from Muskingum College entertain the youngsters with an ever-changing program, and they in turn respond with singing and skits.

Children ten years old and above find fraternal associations as members of a special 4-H club chapter, and their yearly projects in this organization are judged and entered in the district displays at the Muskingum County Fair.

Movies come in for their share of attention also. The home owns a 16mm sound projector, and each week an educational feature is shown. Likewise, Zanesville theater managers have made a standing practice of issuing free group passes to the institute when appropriate plays are being issued, and in many cases have even furnished bus transportation to and from the city.

Each year the Veterans of Foreign Wars invite the lads and lassies in to view the parade, then treat them to luncheon and a show.

Religion Not Neglected

Religious training is never neglected. Grace is said over every meal, and regular Bible study is encouraged, although not forced. All children attend the Fair Oaks Baptist Church Sunday School and morning service each week, and the church furnishes locomotion means from and to the home. The children may attend other churches if relatives or friends secure permission from Mr or Mrs Lane the only home regulation being that there is attendance at some holy meet.

As everywhere, Christmas is the biggest day of the year "down Avondale Way." Each department has a tree of its own, and the superintendant buys and furnishes a present for every charge under his care, augmenting his own funds with contributions from interested residents throughout the district. Bob McCammon usually stuffs his leaner pants with sofa cushions, and waddles in to play Santa Claus. "It's impossible," says Mrs. Lane, "to keep those sprites in bed after 4 O'clock on that morning." From all this even our disinterested average citizen can see that the woebegone

Kiddies of Avondale and McIntire Homes Extended Invitation to County Fair

A special invitation has been extended by Secretary Howard A. Shipley of the Muskingum county fair board to the kiddies of Avondale and McIntire children's home and to the inmates of the home to attend the fair Wednesday.

Elaborate plans have been made for the entertainment of the kiddies and the fair board will spare no effort to show them a good time. John W. Dulan, superintendent of the county home, will be in charge of conveying the inmates of the home to the fair grounds and conducting a general tour of the exhibits and concessions.

Mr. Shipley is desirous, however, to have some persons interested in civic work, furnish automobiles to convey the children of the two homes to the fair grounds and return. Those interested are asked to communicate with Mr. Shipley at the farm bureau office in the court house.

SHOWERS

Columbus, Aug. 10.—Showers tonight; Wednesday partly cloudy and cooler; showers in south portions.

"little orphan Annie" and her brother "Charlie" never were under such wholesome surroundings as furnished by the directors of the Avondale home. Even and despite this, however, adoption is still the one big desire of every child permanently consigned to its care. Both children and officials seek it for both realize that every growing person needs the individual attention given by a mother and father.

Law forbids soliciting however, so the only procedure is to wait for a proper application. Over 25 have been placed for adoption or in free homes where a couple does not wish to make the connection a permanent legality but are willing to bring up a child so far this year. The rub is, though, that nine of ten applicants demand "their" children be babies, and few are willing to take any over three years of age.

All adoptions are made through a combination of legal applications, investigations as to fitness of the applicant by county authorities and a six-month trial period during, which the child lives with his parents-to-be for adjustment and analysis. At the end of this time the "parents" may decide to keep the child, or may return it to the home.

If adoption is the decision full legal control is signed over to them and neither the former parents nor the probate court has further jurisdiction over the case. The child's new location or the

Campbell To Head Avondale Trustees

Paul Campbell of South Zanesville was elected president of the board of trustees of the Avondale

PAUL CAMPBELL

Children's home at the meeting held at the home Sunday afternoon.

G. E. Wilson of Zanesville Rt. 1 was named vice-president and J. F. Lane, superintendent of the home was renamed secretary. Other members of the board are Miss Dorothy Keyes of 24 Cemetery Drive; Mrs. Fred Phillips of 285 Taylor street and W. L. Harper of near Roseville.

The trustees were recently appointed by the commissioner to succeed members of the board, Ernest B. Graham, Harold V. Tom, Welcome Gillogly and Mrs. Vashti Jones Funk who resigned two weeks ago.

Featuring the meeting also was the discussion of affairs pertaining to the home.

Above
Newspaper article, January 8, 1945.

Right
Newspaper ad, October, 1926.

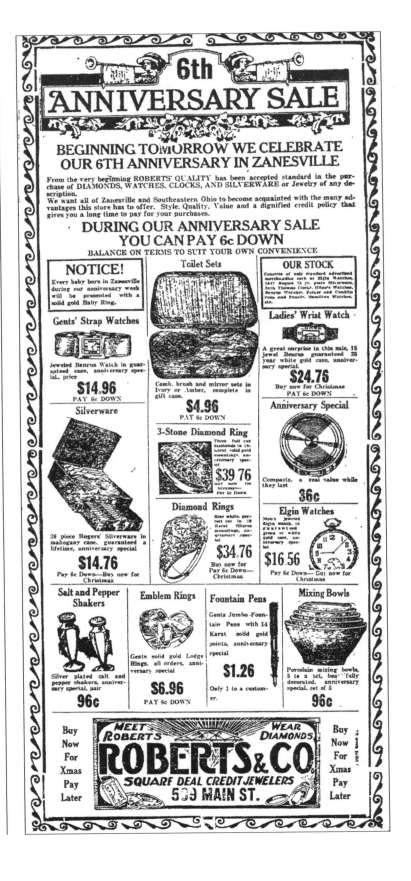

60

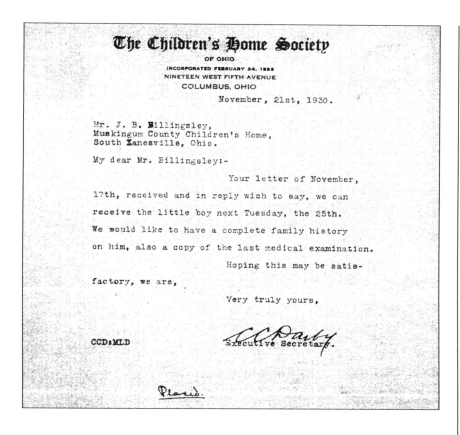

The Children's Home Society
OF OHIO
INCORPORATED FEBRUARY 24, 1883
NINETEEN WEST FIFTH AVENUE
COLUMBUS, OHIO

November, 21st, 1930.

Mr. J. B. Billingsley,
Muskingum County Children's Home,
South Zanesville, Ohio.

My dear Mr. Billingsley:-

Your letter of November, 17th, received and in reply wish to say, we can receive the little boy next Tuesday, the 25th. We would like to have a complete family history on him, also a copy of the last medical examination.

Hoping this may be satisfactory, we are,

Very truly yours,

C. C. Darby
Executive Secretary.

CCD:MLD

Placed.

Left
A request, in writing, from the Children's Home Society of Columbus, Ohio, to receive (place) a little boy from the Avondale Home. No details were found as to why the little boy was being m oved from his hometown of Zanesville to Columbus. The letter is dated November 21, 1930.

name of its foster parents are never revealed to any parent that may be living, though records are kept in order that the child may trace its own origin if it so desires upon reaching maturity.

Mr. and Mrs. Lane have held their positions for over 5 years now and say they hope to be there "as long as there are children who need us and our own ships hold out" Mr. Lane served on the board of trustees before assuming his position, and taught school for 11 years previous to this. He was a farm boy "born and raised" in Muskingum County.

Mrs. Louise Lane also served an apprenticeship in school-work, but was born in Union County. She is a graduate of Wittenberg College. The superintendent's job is one allotted by the board of trustees, subject absolutely to rulings of the state civil service board. Mr. and Mrs. Lane earned their position by means of an intensive examination taken in competition with 13 other couples who applied for the work when the vacancy occurred.

There Mr. Average citizen, is your "Orphan Joe" story still disinterested?

From the Sunday Times-Signal, December 3, 1939.

AND THE RACE GROWS HOTTER

Since calling attention of the voters a few days ago, to the strenuous effort that is being made to re-elect Probate Judge Baker over Attorney Homer Walters, The Signal has had considerable amusement listening to the comments of many who were not aware that such a stiff fight existed at the polls this year. While much of it has favored the present incumbent there is considerable opposition which is rapidly pledging its support to Walters after certain conditions in the county are made known.

Walters although untried at the probate court bench, is given great credit for the efficient administration of municipal court where he has presided many times during the absence of Judge William Freilich. On some occasions Judge Freilich has been forced to vacate his bench for weeks at a time and Walters has very capably filled his duties, meanwhile gaining an enviable record. His campaign for the probate court bench is being based solely on his years of service in the community as a counsellor-at-law and the knowledge of him and faith in his sincerity of administration the voters of city and county hold. More and more are rallying to his standards daily and it looks like a nip-and-tuck race to the very finish as Judge Baker has the strong support of the Black political faction in whose wigwam he has risen to high position.

Baker is meeting his strongest opposition in the county for his conduct of the county school board fight which has precipitated the unpleasant situation regarding the legality of Superintendent F. D. Ring's appointment. He ousted Carl Vandenbark from the school board during the court contest and replaced him with F. C. Whartenby whose political faith demanded the removal of Superintendent Ring, already accepted and certified, and replacement with Charles Westcott of Chandlersville. Thus, was started a fight which has made Muskingum county the laughing stock of the state and so incensed the majority of Muskingum county taxpayers that the continuance of Judge Baker in office is seriously threatened. School supplies were held up for weeks and Superintendent Ring's salary has also been withheld, despite the fact he is substantiated in office by decisions of Attorney General Gilbert Bettman and County Prosecutor C. S. Leasure. Ring, however, has endeavored to do his best under the circumstances to keep school affairs active and has graciously gone about the faithful performance of his duties against such obstacles as certain politically-inclined members of the board have raised. It is not because of any action on the part of Judge Baker to alleviate matters, but solely because of the efforts of Superintendent Ring, that classes are being conducted at all, and the rural voters are intending to demonstrate their animosity at the polls.

The Black faction is particularly anxious to keep Judge Baker in office as the position of probate judge offers about the best opportunity in the county to make contacts and build up a political machine, and it is also no hidden fact that the faction leaders want to oust the management of Avondale Children's home for other reasons that are purely political. Such welfare institutions should be kept above the stench of politics and one visit to the home is sufficient to convince voters of the capabilities of the management there. It would be a safe venture to say that if the little inmates there were allowed to decide control of the Avondale Home it would be an overwhelming vote in favor of continuing the present regime. Who should be better satisfied in a case like this than the pitied orphans themselves?

While there is no concentrated move in the Dresden-Trinway-Frazeysburg section it is hinted by various residents there that an opposition vote is also arising from needy unemployed in the communities who were not given work on the newly constructed highway project, while men from Zanesville were favored. Judge Baker as chairman of the charity committee who recommended workers' names to the contractor, is accused of neglecting many of the local needy.

So, all in all, the race is hotly contested. The charges being mentioned against Judge Baker about equalize the strong support the Black faction is giving him to make the race with Attorney Homer Walters an intensely interesting one which can hardly be settled until the final vote has been officially tabulated.

The Alphabet Prayer

Christian religious learning and an emphasis on personal spirituality was a major component of the intervention strategy present at the earliest years of existence of the Avondale Children's Home. Children and families who were experiencing pain, dysfunction, and loss were to be immersed in a heavy dose of Christian education. It was felt that by being saved as a faithful believer in the salvation provided by the blood of Jesus Christ, the child residents at Avondale would, in turn, save their worldly lives and secure a more hopeful, prosperous future for themselves. Most, if not all, records retrieved from the early years of the Avondale Children's Home shows quite intentionally documented accounts of church attendance, vacation bible school attendance, and Christian baptismal records.

Bible versus were taught to all children residents by the first matron, Mrs. Billingsley, and were said in unison every morning prior to breakfast. The children would stand next to their assigned breakfast chair and repeat the following alphabet prayer:

A…Ask and you shall receive

B…Bless thy soul and forget not all thy benefits

C…Create in me a clean heart, O God

D…Do unto others as they would do unto you

E…Even Christ pleased not himself

F…Forgive us our debts as we forgive our debtors

G…Give us this day our daily bread

H…He that cometh unto me, I will in no wise cast out

I…I am the way, the truth, and the life

J…Jesus today, tomorrow, and forever

K…Keep thy tongue from evil

L…Little children, love one another

M…My son, give me thine heart

N…Now is the accepted time; now is the day of salvation

O…Oh, that men may praise the Lord for His goodness

P…Pray without ceasing

Q…Quit ye like men; be strong

R…Remember the Sabbath to keep it holy

Bible Verses

My son, Keep thy father's commandment, and forsake not the law of thy mother.
Proverbs 6:20

Follow me and I will make you fishers of men.
Matthew 4:19

Blessed are the peacemakers, for they shall be called children of God.
Matthew 5:9

Suffer little children, and forbid them not to come unto me, for such is the kingdom of heaven.
Matthew 20:14

Whosoever shall receive one of these children in my name, receiveth me, and whosoever shall receive me, receive not me, but him that sent me.
Mark 9:37

I am the good shepherd, the good shepherd gives up his life for his sheep.
John 10:11

Children's children are the crown of old men, and the glory of children are their fathers.
Proverbs 17:6

The just man walketh in his integrity, his children are blessed after him.
Proverbs 20:7

Even a child is known by his doings, whether his work be pure, and whether it be right.
Proverbs 20:11

Learn to do well, seek judgement, relieve the oppressed, judge the fatherless, plead for the widow.
Isaiah 1:17

For a good tree bringeth forth not corrupt fruit, neither does a corrupt tree bring forth good fruit.
Luke 6:43

"Betty became the protector of all of her younger siblings who were all at Avondale. Betty loved to make home-made bread. She was a great cook who actually got the "cooking bug" while at Avondale. She was always helping around the kitchen. She would beg to let her work the kitchen detail. Almost every night, the younger kids who would get scared and couldn't sleep would crawl in bed with you if you were older and viewed as a kind person. Betty did not like the fish that was served at Avondale every Friday evening."

Betty Jones – 1938-46
(as told by Betty's daughters, Barbara Parmer and Billie Young).

S...Suffer little children to come unto me, and forbid them not, for such is the kingdom of Heaven

T...Teach me thy way, Oh Lord

U...Unto Thee will I give thanks

V...Verily, I say unto thee, he that believeth in me shall never die

W...Watch and pray, know ye not the day the Lord cometh

X...Xamine your hearts

Y...Ye are bought with a price

Z...Zion be praised

This alphabet prayer was recounted from memory by a former resident, Geneva (LeMaster) Reed and corroborated by other former residents of the era.

Freedom to practice one's personal faith remains a strong principle of intervention to this very day. Whether a child has faith or believes in Jesus Christ as Lord and Savior, or calls his/her God, Lord, Yawhew, Jehovah, Allah, Buddha; the allowance and encouragement to practice one's personal faith is absolute.

Children and the families that they matriculate from have an exceptionally wide range of religious and spiritual beliefs. Some are agnostic or even atheistic; most all Christian religious denominations have been and are represented and we have had child residents who practice Judaism and a recent (2009) practicing Muslim.

Right
Newspaper ad from the *Zanesville Signal*, 1931.

Children Are Taken to Avondale Home

Four children of James Sparks, 70, colored, of near Sonora, were admitted to the Avondale children's home Wednesday, being taken there by Probation Officer Tom Barrett and officers of the home.

Sparks will be moved to the Muskingum county infirmary Thursday, it is said, and three grown daughters will seek work in the community. Death of Mrs. Sparks recently brought about the breaking up of the family, it is said.

Left
Newspaper clipping from the *Times Recorder*, July 20, 1933. The passing of a mother and the moving of an elderly father (70-years-old) to the county infirmary precipitated the placement of these four children.

OFFICIALS PAY VISIT TO AVONDALE HOME

County Commissioners W. S. Osborne, W. R. Burckholter and Elias Kincheloe, Probate Judge John P. Baker and County Engineer George R. Evans were dinner guests Thursday at the Avondale Children's Home. They made an inspection of the home and were profuse in their praise of the services of Mr. and Mrs J. H. Billingsley, superintendent and matron of the home.

At the present time 144 children are being taken care of at the Avondale home and the visitors made the inspection for the purpose of determining what might be needed at the home and what plans could be made to take care of any necessities.

Left
Newspaper clipping from the *Zanesville Signal*, April 3, 1931.

CHAPTER 3

Mid-Century Memories

❖

Memories are what have made Avondale more than just a facility. Each child that lived at Avondale has had countless experiences both good and bad. These memories can be joyful, but in some cases they may be haunting and painful. Sometimes the meaning of those experiences may not be fully understood or contemplated until late into adulthood. Almost always the memories only reflect a snapshot of what happened. In preparing for the 100th anniversary of Avondale, we spoke to many staff and residents.

Once we located past residents, it was not uncommon to find that many of them had been guarded about their Avondale days. Often times, their children or grandchildren would know that they once lived in the home, but wouldn't know much else. It wasn't something spoken of, and in the grand scheme of life little significance was placed on their time in the home. Some may compare it to a veteran who doesn't speak of the war. They may have witnessed horrible atrocities, or shared experiences that just can't be put into words serving them justice. Usually the reason for going to live in a group home is not a happy one. Questioning or trying to understand why it happened may dredge up feelings that many prefer not to revisit. It may be that speaking of such things also means speaking about some pretty intense feelings, which is not easy for most people. Especially those who have experienced a lot of hurt, and may not have had the support or love of a traditional family.

There can be a stigma attached that living in a group home meant that you were no good, an unwanted orphan or a delinquent

Opposite Page
Movie star, Tim Holt visiting the Avondale children in the 1950s.

Above
Advertisement featuring Tim Holt, starring in a movie by Zanesville's own Zane Grey.

"I remember when 'Atomic' the mule treed our brother, Bob, who was trying to eat the green apples from the orchard. We had to chase Atomic away and save our brother. That mule sure could be stubborn and mean!"

Bernie Hamilton – 1941-50

Above
Newspaper ad from the *Zanesville Signal*, 1950.

and sadly some have succumbed to this belief. However, many of the people we spoke with were proud of the obstacles that they had overcome, and had worked hard, enjoyed successful careers and raised loving families. Obviously there were many who chose not to come forward and share their memories of Avondale. We respect their privacy and their reasons for doing so. Some memories are just too personal to share, and certainly not all memories are good ones.

Creating opportunities for people to visit, and hopefully to reconnect with other people seemed important. Avondale has an open door policy, and many people will just show up and ask to look around or visit the cemetery. The request is always honored. We began to find that many people did not know if it was ok to come back, or simply didn't feel comfortable asking. Our desire to learn more about the history of Avondale led us to search out and invite some of the early residents to join us and talk about their experiences. We really had no idea if there would be any interest or if we could even find anyone who lived there prior to the 1970's. However, it wasn't long before they began to come forward. The need for residents to come together became very clear, and as a result we worked to provide opportunities.

Events such as the Avondale Christmas Celebration and the Reunion Picnic have led to some very powerful moments. Several people chose to bring their children and grandchildren to the Christmas Celebration to share a piece of their life that they had never fully revealed. It's difficult to describe the profound impact of such a moment. Imagine having kept a large part of your childhood bottled up, and decades pass by without ever returning to your childhood home. Then one day late in life a time comes when your children and grandchildren join with you to celebrate Christmas in the same place you did as a young child. They get to hear stories about swiping apples from the kitchen, lessons learned and living with dozens of other children in the very place that you stand now.

For some, talking about Avondale was a chance to put that time in their life in context. Being removed from home, and placed in a children's home could feel like a big piece of a person's childhood was taken away, and no one can argue with that. However, in sharing those memories most seemed to find that the space from which something was taken was not empty. The experience may

Hoppy and Three Zanesville Friends

25 MAY 1950 Signal

not have been what they expected or hoped for, but it had affected their lives and they had built relationships that were often not forgotten. Sharing those experiences with their peers, and those of us who were eager to hear seemed to fill a void for many.

So, that is how many of these memories came to be printed on these pages. As with anything that happened in childhood, recollections change and distort. Many people have come back and talked about the long walk to the laundry building only to realize it is just a few yards away. Others remember mopping the very long hallway between the boys and girls side and are startled by how short it actually is in reality. Some insist that the dining room was bigger in the old days, but the truth is that their childhood eyes were just much smaller.

Above
Mrs. Mildred Way's boys and girls.

Avondale – The Farm

During the early, formative years of the Avondale Children's Home, creature comforts were exceedingly rare, available resources were scarce, and the work that was needed to be accomplished in order to maintain the Children's Home was very difficult. Much of the work necessary to accomplish the noble mission at the Avondale Children's Home was either accomplished in total or in part by the residents of the home. Eventually, running a fully functioning, virtually self-sufficient farm-type operation required daily attention and much active labor. The children, sometimes with and many times without, adult supervision were responsible for the planting of crops, harvesting of the same crops, milking the cows, feeding the horses and mules, taking further care of all livestock, food preparation, darning and knitting, maintenance and upkeep of the surrounding grounds, cleaning the physical facility, and much more. The work was never easily accomplished and was, in a quite literal sense, never ending.

One resident recalls, "In the forties, they got rid of the two big workhorses, Bob and Tom, and got a Farmall Super A Tractor. The farmer, Louie Ayers was a horse man, and he never learned to drive. All his life he used horses. I learned to drive a tractor and a car when I was eleven years old. I was a kid trying to teach Louie about the clutch, and brake and how to use them together and all that stuff. So one day I said to Louie, I'm going to go open up this gate, and you can bring the tractor through the gate. There used to be fencing all through the grounds back by the old barn. All of a sudden I hear the tractor coming behind me and old Louie is saying, "Wo! Wo! Wo!" like he's trying to stop a horse! I jumped out of the way and he went right through that gate".

Many times, local residents including farmers, under the guise of "adopting" a young boy or girl, would use their able bodies to accomplish work tasks on their farms or homes and, once these work tasks were accomplished, relinquish their rights to "adoption." One former anonymous resident from the 1940's era recalls such a situation.

"Sometime in the forties I had a home visit at Arch Springs Farm, and I worked from before daylight till after dark. They fed me good there, but they would send me in from the fields and say while you're resting go ahead and mow the lawn. I had some kind of a stroke maybe a sun stroke or regular stroke but they took

"All of us kids, Bob, Bernie, Charles, Frankie, and Margie arrived in 1941. We were separated by gender when we arrived at Avondale…girls one way…boys the other way. The boys were all so scared that we were all hanging onto each other, just like a little train, because we were so scared. All of the other boys were looking at us like 'Don't be such babies.'"

Bernie Hamilton – 1941-50

me right back to the home as soon as that happened and I was in bed for about two months. I was probably 12 years Old. Farmers would take the kids and say various things about adopting you, work you to death and at the end of farm season they would take you back. In the old days it was tough".

It is unclear when Avondale ceased its farm operation. It seems likely that it was in the very early 1950's. Perhaps, it was no longer practical to rely on farm produce, or it became too expensive to farm rather than to get food by other means. It may be just as likely that Food & Drug Administration regulations and nutritional requirements made it impossible to operate the farm. In any case, Avondale would never again have hundreds of chickens, or fields of corn as it once did.

Resident Bernie Hamilton Recalls:

Jesse Hutson taught school at the schoolhouse, but when Fred Lane left, Jesse took the superintendent job. Jesse was a tall slim man with grey hair parted down the center.

Jesse could get mean. A job like that could be stressful, but he could be pretty mean. The matron's didn't have a paddle, they would just smack you on the side of the head. It would make your

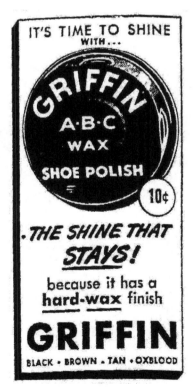

Right

Heartbreaking yet necessary actions continue to be accomplished; all to ensure the safety and protection of children. Charles and Bernie lit the Christmas tree at the 2010 Avondale Christmas celebration and have frequently attended reunion events.

Below

Giant Baby Ruth candy bar was a big hit for children at the Avondale Home, May 7, 1953.

YOUNGSTERS at Avondale Children's home are in for a treat, thanks to the Kroger supermarket here.

The local store now has on display a giant size Baby Ruth candy bar more than four feet in length and 15 inches thick which will be given to the youngsters on May 18.

But while the big bar is on display, the Kroger store has arranged for a contest with the winners receiving a Therma-King portable ice box.

The prizes will be awarded to the two persons who guess closest in ounces the weight of the candy bar. No purchases at the store are necessary but entry blanks are available there.

Here a father, forced to let the county care for his five children, holds the youngest as the others lineup beside him. Left to right are Charles, Robert. William. and Maxine Hamilton, and Frankie with his father, Wilbur Hamilton.

Five Children Become Wards Of County By Ruling of State

Mother To Be Taken to Columbus; Father, a Relief Client, Parts From Them

Muskingum county today was preparing to assume care of five youngsters, ranging from two to 10 years of age.

Their mother, 33, is in custody at women's quarters of county jail awaiting removal to the Ohio State hospital for the insane at Columbus.

Their father, a man of 55 and a resident of Cumberland, parted with the children after attempting five months to give them proper home care and parental assistance. He is a Muskingum county relief client.

The kiddies are Charles Edward Hamilton, 10; Robert Stanley Hamilton, 8; William Bernard Hamilton, 6; Maxine Alberta Hamilton, 4, and Frankie Thomas Hamilton, aged 2. They are children of Mr. and Mrs. Wilbur Hamilton, of Cumberland, Guernsey county.

SCHOOL STUDENTS

Charles Edward, Robert Stanley, and William Bernard Hamilton had been students at Cumberland-Spencer consolidated school at Cumberland and receiving good grades in their class work.

The other two kiddies had been cared for by the father and friends.

Their mother, Mrs. Vera Irene Hamilton, was haled before Noble county probate court at Caldwell last week and after a hearing was ordered committed to the Ohio state asylum. Through conflict in county authority, the Noble county court removed the mother to Muskingum county, instead of the Columbus institution and left her at the Muskingum county jail.

Some time ago the case came to the attention of John King, trustee of Spencer township, Cumberland, Guernsey county. He appealed to Muskingum county probate court to assume care of the kiddies but as the father owned property at Cumberland, the case was referred to the attorney general at Columbus.

ATTORNEY RULES

The attorney general ruled Muskingum county should assume responsibility.

The father formerly owned more than 100 acres of farm land near High Hill but sold it about 18 months ago. He said his wife no longer would live on the farm.

With part of the proceeds, he purchased property at Cumberland but it is of little or no value, a county official said today. Hamilton for the past 52 years has been handicapped with a withered right hand and arm, the result of infantile paralysis when he was a child.

He has been unable to work sufficiently to support the family and most of the funds received from sale of the farm have been used for household expenses.

Hamilton said his wife left home last May and returned to her former home at Caldwell. He said since that time he had been attempting to keep his kiddies home but was forced to give up the task and place the kiddies at Avondale Children's home.

Youngsters at Avondale Children's Home got their fill of candy yesterday, thanks to the Kroger company which presented them with this bar weighing 1,648 ounces. David Bowers, second from left, looks as though he's ready to eat his share of the gift. Others left to right are Melvin Bosze, Eddie Miller, Richard Bowers, Sam Rickett and Bill Kuhn.

ears ring, and if you were little it could knock you down. If they told you something you better do it.

If you had trouble with a Matron they would report you to Jesse. You would get sent to the front office next to the main doors. There was a big desk that they would lay you across, and a great big paddle used to hang on wall. You'd get a lickin' so bad you'd beg 'em to quit. Then their favorite thing to say was, "If you don't behave yourself we'll send you to The Boys Industrial School in Lancaster". One time I was working as the kitchen boy. I just got done and walked into the boys side. Jesse was sitting there and said, "Come here Hamilton, one of the cooks said you got mad and slammed the door because you had to be kitchen boy". I barely got a word out and he just lit into me and wouldn't quit. He about tore my head off and wouldn't quit. He just wouldn't quit. I was about 8 or 9 years old.

We went there November 11, 1941 and it was probably the best thing that ever happened to us. We were so poor. I remember that day walking into the home my two older brothers in front of me, my sister and the baby behind me. We were all holding on to each other, scared to death with all the kids looking us over. I remember the day before we were out behind the outhouse playing in the mud making mud pies. That's when my Dad came out and told us that he was taking us all to the home tomorrow. All of us kids started crying. Some of us were old enough to know what that meant but not all of us. We never dreamed that would happen to us, and it was a shock. In those days they broke you up from your brothers and sisters, and never told you where they went. They would often change their names and never tell them they were adopted. Some of them ended up getting adopted. We had a sister that we didn't see for nearly 30 years. She had been told that she was adopted, but our baby brother never knew. We found him but he didn't believe us and wouldn't have anything to do with us. He has since passed away.

I remember Louie Ayers was the farmer, and when you got old enough you would help Louie with the farm work. I remember walking behind the team of horses all day long as a young boy in the hot sun. He was a good old guy. He stayed in the apartment over the laundry, and Jesse's family lived in the upstairs of the main building.

At Avondale, you were just a number while we were there. We

Above
A true to life celebrity arrives for a long term stay at Avondale Youth Center.

"The day Atomic was delivered to Avondale, the boys were all lined up in a row and whoever Atomic stopped walking in front of, that boy was responsible for all of his care, including feeding. You were in charge of Atomic for an entire month. Atomic was certainly mean and if he was in a certain mood, he would kick or throw you every time!"

Charles Hamilton – 1941-50

Above
Newspaper clipping, July 10, 1954.

Above
A young boy stands on the Avondale grounds just to the west of the baseball diamonds.

were well cared for though. We had clothes, food and somewhere to sleep.

Times were so hard there weren't many people who could or wanted to adopt kids.

I remember when the water tower caught on fire. Someone put an oil stove in it to keep lines from freezing and it caught on fire.

We got Atomic the Mule at Christmas time and kept him in the orchard. My brother would tease Atomic, and one time that mule got him cornered up in a tree and wouldn't let him down. That mule could be mean.

We found out one of the boys was tattling to the Matron about some things. So one night we got him after dark and tied him to a tree. Then we threw cow manure all over him.

One boy got caught stealing a jar of peanut butter. So the next day at dinner they made him eat the whole jar.

I remember when they first got a tractor, old Louie Ayers had farmed with horses for 50 or 60 years. He would get on that tractor and yell Whoa! Whoa! "Louie that's a tractor you gotta push the brake, it ain't no horse!"

At Christmas time you might get a windup toy, some new overalls and a shirt.

Once a year we would go to the fair. Sometimes we would go to Moxahala Park and go skating. They also would have shows there-magicians, knife throwers, etc.

In the winter time when it got really cold we would get five gallon buckets of water and pour it down the driveway. When it would freeze we would ride our sleds down across the road and clear down to the creek. We made sling shots out of old inner tubes and had corn cob fights.

This was toward the end of the depression era, and there still wasn't any work. The bums and hobos were bad in those days, the roads were full of them. They would come up to the building and the home would feed them. They would tell us about their experiences. We always thought those hobos were neat. They'd tell stories about places they'd been and how to make mulligan stew. During the war they were around all the time, back when there weren't any cars on the road. The hobos would tell each other where to stop to get a free meal. The home became one of

'Mom' Of Hundreds Retires

Mrs. Mary Hoppstatter is afraid she's going to be very lonesome soon, as she is leaving the home where she has enjoyed many of her several hundred "daughters," and the job at which she sometimes worked around the clock.

For Mrs. Hoppstatter is leaving the Avondale Children's home where she has been house mother of the girls for the past 10 years.

She is retiring next Saturday and plans to take a rest since she will be 71 years old on Feb-ruary 9, 1955. After she takes that rest, she's not sure just what she will do. But for the present, she plans to live in an apartment on South Sixth street.

Mrs. Hoppstatter isn't sure how many girls she has mothered in her 10 years at the home. But she says they have ranged in age from tiny tots nursed by bottles to Lucille Lampros who became the bride of Edward Canter in the Rolling Plains Methodist church last Sunday night.

In caring for the girls, small and large, she has been all that a mother should be. She nursed them through outbreaks of measles, chicken pox and the other ailments of childhood; their bruises and scratches and was their counselor through the teen age years.

She remembers how the girls have come, grown up and left over the decade she has been at the home, and apparently most of them remember her too for she always receives a host of cards and gifts at Christmas time, and some for her birthday, from her former "daughters." And quite often the boys and girls who leave return for a visit "back home" and they always look in on their friend of the years when they were growing up.

It was in July of 1944 that Mrs. Hoppstatter went to work at the home. She had been alone since Oct. 23, 1940 when her husband, Charles died at their home on Forest avenue. Her daughter had married and when she went to work for Mr. and Mrs. Fred Lane at Avondale, she found caring for the youngsters kept her busy and happy.

She stayed at the home during the administration of Mr. and Mrs. Jesse Hutson and now regrets leaving Mr. and Mrs. Jack Caughey, the present superintendent and matron, as well as the children.

Her hours of work, she says, have sometimes been long, when youngsters were ill or had a toothache or earache. She worried as any mother would and

(Turn to Page 3, Please)

PARTING SOON—Mrs. Mary Hoppstatter, center, will soon be parting from her many "daughters" as she is leaving the Avondale Children's home where she has been house mother for girls for the past 10 years. Shown seated with her are Rosemary Rognan and Lois Billingsley while standing at her side are Juanita Bowers and Ruth Lanning.

'Mother' Of Hundreds Retires

(Continued from Page 1)
comforted them, and rejoiced with them in their pleasures. She attended church and Sunday school with her "daughters" and saw to it they were all dressed and ready when it came time to go to school. She sometimes helped them with their studies, and personal problems too, as they grew older.

The pre-school children were a bigger part of her work, for they were around on school days when most of the others were in classes.

On alternate week ends she was off duty, and these she spent with her daughter, Mrs. Kenneth Wright, and grandchildren, Marilyn Wright, 18 and Richard, 14, at their home on Euclid avenue. When the Wright children were young, they frequently spent week ends at "the home" at Avondale, just to be with Grandma.

Now that she has given notice she is retiring from the Avondale home, Mrs. Hoppstatter is beginning to wonder just how lonesome it is going to be without her "daughters." But she has one consolation — Zanesville isn't far from Avondale and if she gets too lonesome she'll be able to go back "home" for a visit.

Left and Above
Newspaper clipping from the *The Times Recorder*, July 10, 1954. Mrs. Hoppstatter, who retired at age 71, was one of many people to greatly impact those at Avondale.

the places they knew they could stop. One old hobo came up, and all of us kids were looking at him. He had a pearl handled revolver sticking out of his back pocket.

There used to be a program called relief where once a month you could come to town and get food, but a lot of people didn't have cars so they would leave the day before and walk to town. My dad used to leave the night before and he might get a ride or he might not. He was crippled so he did the best he could. Then he'd be back in two or three days with some food.

Above

Young men and a young woman pose for a picture inside of the foyer at the Avondale Children's Home.

Right

Compare the Children's Home budget of $45,250.41 in April of 1954 to the Avondale Youth Center budget of $1,574,163.74 during the calendar year of 2010.

Welfare: Civilian Defense:		
Salary, Director	$	960.00
Compensation Employes		1,800.00
Stationery & Supplies		482.05
Other Expenses		16.83
Total Civilian Defense	$	3,258.88
Charities:		
County Home:		
Salaries, Superintendent & Matron	$	4,020.00
Compensation Employes		42,277.75
Physician's Salary		750.00
Fuel & Light		4,055.22
Maintenance Supplies		9,697.91
Farm Supplies		2,169.59
Repairs		1,868.15
Other Expenses, Drugs, Burials, etc.		6,658.98
New Equipment		3,921.39
Total County Home	$	75,418.99
Child Welfare Board:		
Salaries, Sec'y & Investigator	$	5,880.00
Maintenance of Children in Other Homes		17,928.11
Other Expenses—Stationery, Mileage, etc.		1,131.59
Total Child Welfare	$	24,939.70
Children's Home:		
Salary, Superintendent & Matron	$	4,020.00
Compensation Employes		12,762.70
Fuel & Light		2,009.73
Maintenance & Supplies		12,788.48
Farm Supplies		2,088.08
Repairs		2,823.55
Other Expenses		4,988.24
New Equipment		2,987.51
Construction		782.12
Total Children's Home	$	45,250.41
Soldiers Relief & Burials:		
Compensation Members Relief Commission	$	2,280.00
Compensation, Investigators & Clerks		6,327.50
Other Expenses, Stationery, etc.		1,018.03
Grants—Soldiers, Sailors, Widows & Children		26,405.00
Markers for Graves		85.50
Memorial Day Expenses		555.00
Burials		500.00
Burial Fees—Committee		10.00
Total Soldiers Relief & Burials	$	37,181.03
Juvenile Detention Home:		
Salary, Superintendent & Matron	$	2,256.00
Compensation Employes		1,020.00
Maintenance—Meals, etc.		1,548.50
Other Expenses		153.79
Total Detention Home	$	4,978.29

1941-1950 Memories 'Anonymous':

One day I remember the kids were behind the pump house at the back steps making mud pies. There was one kid for a lookout. I was there but wasn't even involved in it. All of sudden the lookout yells, "hear she comes!" Here came Mrs. Lane. The other kids took off, but I hadn't done anything so I just stood there. Mrs. Lane didn't say a word she just started beating me with a 2x4. They meant business in the old days.

I used to take care of that old cemetery. I would clean it up for Memorial Day, but hardly anyone ever brought out flowers.

There was a comedian who was pretty popular that gave us a Mexican Mountain Burro. It looked something like a donkey, but had wee little hooves. They lined all us kids up and asked us what we would name him. Someone came up with the name 'Atomic', like the Atomic Bomb. And that thing was an Atomic Bomb. He said, we're going to let him go and whoever he stops in front has to take care of him. Who do you think he stopped in front of? He stopped and nuzzled me, like he liked me. It was the meanest damn thing you ever seen! First thing I did was put him in the stall. I came in and he tried to kick me to death. You couldn't trust him. Kids would try to ride him and he would gallop along, and all of a sudden put his head down, kick his legs out and you'd slide right off. You never knew what he was going to do. There was a girl named Louise riding him one day and he bucked her right off!

We went by rates. The first rate was yard boy, which I was at 9 years old. You went outside and picked up sticks. Then you went to mower boy in the summer, and mowed with the old style manual mower. Then you went inside and became dormitory boy, and made beds and stuff like that. Then you became kitchen boy and worked the potato peeler and other kitchen chores. Then I went to Barn boy and milked and fed cows morning, night and even before school. There were three of us and I eventually became head barn boy, so the other boys worked for me.

One day during the war we were playing B-17 bomber in the apple tree and I was the pilot. Mrs. Lane caught us. The standard punishment for doing something like that, which really you could only hurt yourself, but to her was a great crime, was two weeks on the bench. There were two great big long benches in the living room. You could get permission to go to the bathroom, and to bed but otherwise you sat on that bench.

One day me and some of the other boys were playing, and running around near the bathroom. I went around the corner and slid and skinned my leg up. I got an infection that got real bad. Mrs. Lane took me upstairs and put me in one of those rooms. I remember that because her daughter was up there, she lived with them at the time and went to High School. Mrs. Lane probably saved my leg. She covered my leg with a cloth and then poured boiling hot water on it. It wasn't too bad because of the cloth but it was really either get scalded with water or suffer the infection. When you go through something like that, you don't forget it till the day you die.

A lot of people used to say the kids out there come from trash and don't amount to nothin'. I'm not one of them. I don't believe

Above
Child playing on the playground equipment at the Avondale Children's Home.

Sertoma Club Meets At Avondale Home

Members of the Sertoma club held their dinner meeting last night at the Avondale Children's Home and came close to being defeated in a softball game played with a boys' team from the home.

Kenneth Swope hit a home run with the bases loaded in the last inning to put the men ahead, 10 to 9.

The chicken dinner was served buffet style on the lawn in front of the home. Richard Riebau is president of the club.

Above
Newspaper clipping, July 28, 1954.

in that because a lot of those kids were smart. It wasn't our fault we were out there. I was in the service. I left Avondale and the same day I enlisted in the Navy. I was the first Commander of our VFW post. I was a supervisor at the city for 20 years. One boy Charlie Rodman became a music professor at the University of Arizona.

Resident Jacqueline (Jackie) Jones Recalls:

I became a resident of the Avondale Children's Home in December of 1956. My parents divorced a couple of years before that and my mom was forced to go to work to help make ends meet. At that time, I became a domestic engineer at the age of 12. I was cleaning the house, doing the laundry on a wringing washer and hanging the clothes on the outside clothesline, cooking meals and if that wasn't enough, I took care of my four siblings.

Through all of that there wasn't much of a chance to be a pre-teen so I began to rebel and finally got their attention. So my brother and I went to live with our Grandparents to help alleviate some of the financial burden. Two months later Grandma passed away in her sleep. My brother was placed in a foster home and I went to the Children's Home, as Grandpa was unable to care for us the way he worked.

Actually the situation was the best thing that ever happened to me. I finally was allowed to be a teenager for the first time. It was two weeks before Christmas, I was still mourning the loss of my Grandma and then being away from home for the first time it was a little difficult to settle in and adjust. Once I settled in it was like living with 23 big and little sisters.

I learned discipline and structure. Our day started at 6:00 a.m. on school days and 7:00 a.m. on weekends, holidays and summer vacations and the day ended with bedtime at 9:30 and 10:00 p.m.

Upon rising, we made our bed, dressed and then had breakfast. After breakfast, we did our chores; such as, dusting, mopping, cleaning the bathrooms, cleaning the dining room, and doing dishes all before getting ready for school. On Saturday the chores were a lot more serious cleaning. The chores were rotated on a weekly basis so you didn't get bored of doing the same job. In the summer, we washed walls and cleaned windows and even got to try our hand at doing some painting. The work we did was not

Above
Jacqueline (Jackie) Jones, Avondale resident, 1956-1961.

185 Youngsters Supervised By County Welfare Board

There were 185 children under the supervision of the Muskingum County Welfare board at the end of 1957, according to the annual report of Mrs. Lois M. Sneil, executive secretary.

Of the number, 50 live at the Avondale home, 30 are in other institutions, 12 are with parents, 20 with relatives, 69 in boarding homes and four elsewhere.

The board is in its 12th year. Basically, its responsibility is to provide protective service to neglected and dependent children who are committed by Juvenile Court or whose parents or relatives voluntarily ask for service.

The board also assists with crippled and blind children, special class children, adoptions and other types of social investigations. Attention is focused on preventive and non-punitive services in an effort to keep children with their own families and give whatever help is necessary to prevent a child from becoming delinquent.

During 1957, 34 children were committed to the board for supervision by Juvenile Court while 13 others volunteered.

During the same period, 16 were placed in Avondale home, 40 in boarding homes, 16 with relatives, 21 with parents, two in free homes, nine in adoptive homes, seven in other institutions and 21 in special class boarding homes.

The board handled the placement of 35 crippled and four blind children. It made 24 investigations for other welfare agencies and Common Pleas court. It handled 23 reports on adoptions and conducted two investigations for International Social Service relative to adoptions in foreign countries.

Fifty - four cases were closed during the year.

The total cost of the program, including salaries, administration and maintenance of Avondale home, was $88,459.64. Collections from parents, Social Security,

Above
"Danny" the miniature horse pulls a group of Avondale children, in the 1950s. Notice the Muskingum County Children's Home name on the car in the background.

Above
Shirley Gilmore, c. 1950s. In the bottom photo, Shirley is shown holding "hose-nose."

hard and when I got older I realized it only helped prepare me for life.

During the school year we participated in many after school activities-school plays, dances, prom, and went to all the football and basketball games. We were allowed to date (double date) but we seldom did, only on special occasions. There was always a designated time to do homework, after supper and before bedtime and if you were lucky enough to finish early you got to watch a little television before going to bed.

We attended church on Sunday and I was very much involved in the youth group, helped with church suppers, taught a pre-school Sunday School class, and attended church camp in the summer. I still attend the same church - I was married there, had all three of my children baptized there, and my two sons were married there.

In the summer, we went to Lake Isabella to swim a couple times a week, went to the Skyway Drive-in theater, went to the county fair, went camping at Seneca Lake and Pymatuning Lake and like normal teenagers we sunbathed as often as we could.

We got to attend several local functions throughout the year. We went to the Liberty Theater and saw many of the big name movies, like "The Robe" and "The Ten Commandments", went to the Shrine Circus in Columbus, and the Sertomea Pancake Day.

Birthdays were made a very special day with a cake and a gift (purchased by one of the local women organizations). At Christmas, we were asked to make a list of three items we really wanted for Christmas. We got one of the items on the list and them we all got some small things that were bought in bulk; such as: nail polish kits, gloves, slippers, bubble bath, etc. At graduation, we all received a large piece of Samsonite luggage with our initials on it.

The home had a huge room in the basement that was used as a recreation room where we played board games, cards, listened to and danced to the current music on a record player. When the old Avondale School that sat in back of the home closed, it was renovated into a recreational center. A jukebox was donated for us to play the current hits and occasionally we went shopping to update it with the newest hits, and someone gave us a used Ping-Pong table. It was a neat place for entertainment and socializing on Saturday evenings and Sunday afternoon.

My mentor and very special friend was the head cook and she

Above
Newspaper clipping from the *Zanesville Times Recorder,* April 5, 1954.

Above Left
Avondale kids, c. 1950s.

was a die-hard Cleveland Indians fan and listened to them on the radio on Sunday afternoon in the kitchen. Since I liked the Indians too, I always volunteered to help her make sandwiches for the evening meal so I could listen to the game with her.

I got to work part-time jobs to earn extra money to help pay for my class ring, senior year pictures and other extras. I delivered the evening and Sunday morning newspaper, "The Signal". I frequently babysat for a family (she was a former resident) and sometimes helped her with cleaning chores on Saturday. She has been my very best friend all these years. The summer before my senior year I was able to utilize my secretarial skills from school by working at a local real estate office.

My experience of being at the Avondale Children's Home was truly very rewarding. I learned life morals and work ethics from the time I spent there. I developed some very lasting friendships that I have stayed in contact with over the years.

– by Jacqueline (Jackie) Jones

Above
Newspaper ad, 1954.

Above
Several Avondale Children's Home youth in a posed photograph near the barn on the grounds. Picture dated 1959.

Right
Newspaper clipping from March 19, 1953.

Avondale Kiddies Get Pony and Cart

The children at Avondale Home now have a real, live pony and a fancy cart for their personal use. The pony, named "Danny," was presented to the home by Dr. Louis Cassady of Fultonham. The Farm Implement Co. and the Finalw Lumber Co. provided the cart and Bryan's Feed store furnished the harness. In photo, on front seat, left to right, are Elsie Billingsly, Rosemary Rognon and Sharon Spires. Back seat, Jean Crippen, Sue Moore and Barbara Nelson.

Brownie Troop Honors Avondale Youngsters

Members of Brownie Troop No. 36 presented an Easter centerpiece to the children of Avondale home during the week-end under the direction of their leaders, Mrs. William Bee and Mrs. Thomas Darby. In the front row, left to right, are Pamela Waltman, Billie Bee, Vicky Groce, Ruth Truax, Marvilla Harding, Sharon Burke, Marlene Riehl, and Linda Kay Hill. Second row, left to right, are Becky Mc-Donald, Dixie Valentine, Flora Mae Faust, Joanne Darby, Joyce Leasure, and Cindy Sawyer.

Above
Newspaper clipping from the *Zanesville Times Recorder,* April 20, 1954.

Left
Newspaper ad, 1954.

Two Boys and Their Pig Project

Besides cattle, projects, garden entries and sewing projects, kids from the Avondale Home will enter into other activities at the fair. One of these will be a pig project. 11-year-old Bill Kuhn, left, and his partner, Melvin Bozze, age 12, will show these two pigs in the fat barrow class of the junior fair. Both boys are in their second year in 4H and are members of the Rolling Plains 4H Club. All the boys and girls at the home owe a great deal of thanks to Mr. and Mrs. Jack Caughey for the wonderful job they are doing in encouraging the kids to participate in the many youth activities at the fair.

Above

At one time, all forms of farming were present on the Children's Home grounds. Self-sufficiency was the rule of the day. By the 1950s, livestock was primarily for the purposes of "show" through 4H and the county fair.

Kitchen Help Plentiful at Avondale Home

11-29-52

Youngsters at the Avondale Children's home gave the matron, Mrs. John Caughey, little peace this morning as she supervised preparation of Thanksgiving dinner. Chicken headed the menu. With Mrs. Caughey, left to right, are Rosemary Rogman, six; Tim Miller, seven, and Kenneth Miller, six.

Avondale Children Hear Local Judge

Judge Clarence J. Crossland shows copy of Declaration of Independence to Frances Newell, left, and Mary Axline at Avondale Children's home last night where he was the principal speaker at a meeting of the Sertoma club. The jurist spoke on "The Value of Independence" launching the club's drive to acquaint young people with the importance of the document. Similar talks will be made at

Above
And a portrait of resident Bill Kuhn taken in 1954 at age 12.

Above

Bill Kuhn in his high school band uniform, August, 1959. Bill played the trumpet.

Left Top
Newspaper clipping from November 27, 1952.

Left Bottom
Newspaper clipping, date unknown.

Above
John "Pop" Caughey surrounded by kids as he sits on the steps of the schoolhouse, c. 1959.

Right
Newspaper clipping from the *Zanesville Signal* (date unknown), featuring Atomic the donkey with WHIZ announcer Ed Fisher, who would later go on to be "Bozo the Clown" on Cleveland television.

Donkey for Avondale Home Honored by Marine Corps

"Atomic," the donkey won by Ed Fisher, left, was made an honorary sergeant in charge of recreation at Avondale Children's home by Marine Sgt. Ray Pennock, at right.

A small donkey won in a contest by Ed Fisher, announcer at WHIZ, and turned over to the children of Avondale home, was getting acquainted with his newfound friends today.

The donkey was flown from Los Angeles to Cincinnati yesterday and was brought to this city by truck.

Fisher promptly took charge of the animal, later turning it over to Marine Sergeant Ray Pennock of the local recruiting station.

Sgt. Pennock presented the donkey to youngsters of the home during ceremonies last night at the grounds. "Atomic" was made an honorary sergeant in the Marine Corps.

The donkey was accepted by Jesse Hutson, superintendent of the home. The Avonale children sang several songs during the program which was broadcast over WHIZ.

The contest in which Fisher won the prize for submitting the most suitable name for the donkey was sponsored by Jerry Colonna, the radio star who appears regularly with Bob Hope.

Another photo of "Atomic" appears on Page 8.

Avondale Youngsters Guests at Party

Youngsters from Avondale Children's home were guests at a Christmas party last night at Masonic temple, given by members of Cyrene Commandery, Knights Templar. Santa was on hand to distribute gifts. Some of the young guests, left to right, are: Myrtle Shipman, Donna Barker, Larry Kuhn, Terry Warfield, Jo Ann Barker, Dave Barker and Carolyn Gaus. Ronnie Rognon is seated at left.

Left
Newspaper clipping from December 19, 1951. The community's generosity towards Avondale has been a long-standing tradition.

Below
Sun-bathing beauties being watched by young boys at the home.

BLOW, BILL, BLOW!—This isn't Gabriel tooting the trumpet. It's 14-year-old Bill Kuhn, who lives at the Avondale Children's home, attends Rolling Plains school where he's in the eighth grade and that horn is his Christmas gift. It happened this way: Jack Caughey, (looking on with smiles,) superintendent of the home promised Bill would get a horn for Christmas if he could produce a "score card" from school with plenty of A grades. The report card showed just that; Bill has musical talent, and a second-hand trumpet was advertised in the Times-Recorder. Result—Caughey was as pleased as Bill with the report card, the horn was purchased and Bill got his Christmas present ahead of schedule. Other boys and girls at Avondale are also looking to Times Recorder readers for their Merry Christmas gifts

Above
Bill Kuhn and "Pop" Caughey.

Above
Young riders at the Avondale Children's Home enjoying the rural farm environment the home had to offer.

Left
Newspaper ad from the *Zanesville Signal*, 1950.

"Life values acquired at the home...and it was a home to all of us...have guided me throughout my life!"

Bill Kuhn – 1950-61
(Mr. Kuhn has served his country honorably and with dignity as a member of the United States Marine Corps from 1961 to 1981).

CHAPTER 4

Avondale Scrapbook

❖

There has been so much that has happened in 100 years. Those events which were judged as important at the time were often captured in the daily newspaper, or shared by word of mouth. Some events were noteworthy because of achievement or maybe it was a generous donation by a group or an individual. Perhaps the most important events, though, are almost never recorded.

Important moments happen all day long at Avondale every day, and have happened for 100 years. Every day the staff at Avondale place importance on how the kids feel, and what they are thinking or doing. Something as seemingly insignificant as, "Oh, you're hungry? Then let's go make a snack!", shares concern and feeling of warmth that will never make the newspaper. It may seem insignificant, but not to the child who never had food in the house or had to steal from a gas station so their 4-year old brother could eat. Simply taking the time to help a child with a homework assignment lets them know that they are worthy of an adult's time, and that someone believes they are capable. Learning life-skills, getting ready for their first dance or the first Christmas with actual presents can all be amazing moments that most people will not know about or get to share.

The beauty of a scrapbook is that there may or may not be context to what you find. Some of the articles are very clear and to the point. There may be pictures that some find interesting, but to others may have a much deeper meaning or spark some special memory. Every powerful moment cannot be captured, but maybe at least we can catch a glimpse of some of times that have made Avondale special.

Opposite Page Top
Avondale "Kiddies" proudly showing gifts from the Avondale Christmas Fund, 1966.

Opposite Page Bottom Left
Director, Roger Russell kept kids busy with events like the Soapbox Derby, c. 1970s.

Opposite Page Bottom Right
Photo from newspaper with caption reading: "Cindy Russell, Directors' 12-year-old daughter (center), joins Becky Gill, 14, (left) and Mary Fleming, 14, in girl's lounge with Avondale Children's Home two of four dogs Duffy and Old Yellow. Paneled room looks like living room anywhere where television is enjoyed set in the midst of oval Colonial rug matched with furnishings and made comfortable to avoid the look of an institution." December 2, 1973.

"We were like one big happy family!"

Avondale and Roseville Graduates, Class of 1961 – Vivian Truax (Johnson), Jackie Vandenbark-Jones, Bill Kuhn, Beulah Kindes-Strickler.

27 Girls And 26 Boys Share One Home

Muskingum County's "biggest family" consists of 53 boys and girls, all of school age. They play together, work together and eat together. They laugh together and cry together, tussle with each other and defend each other, just like children in smaller families. They live at Muskingum County's Avondale Children's Home.

The "father" and "mother" who listen to their troubles, who cheer them in their adversities, who encourage them in their efforts, and who praise them for their accomplishments are Mr. and Mrs. Jack Caughey, superintendent and matron of the home.

Some of the children are orphans. Others, the greater part, are residents of the home because of marital separations, divorce and neglect in Muskingum County families.

The Avondale children attend the elementary grades at Newton Local School in White Cottage and complete their final classes at Roseville High School.

Sharing the responsibilities of housekeeping for the "biggest family" the foster brothers and sisters have regular chores which they are required to perform before and after school.

Most of the serving at the tables is done by the girls whose principal activities in the kitchen are confined to vegetable preparation and dishwashing. The use of the cooking facilities is made available to the older girls as the need may be occasioned by their home economics classes. Saturday is set aside as a day for general cleaning.

Mrs. Opal Wolfe is house mother of the dorm where the 26 boys sleep in bunk beds. House mother of the dorm which accommodates the 27 girls is Mrs. Leona Settles.

The staff of employes in the maintenance of the home also includes two women in the kitchen, two in the laundry, one housekeeper and one maintenance man. During the vacation season the girls' relief assistance in the laundry gives them an opportunity for practical experience.

Regularity of schedule is the keyword to the discipline in the family. After the evening meal the TV is turned off at 7 o'clock and the study sessions begin. Bedtime for children in the first and second grades is 8 p.m., in the third, fourth and fifth grades it is 8:30, while those preparing lessons for the sixth, seventh and eighth grades study until 9 p.m.

To care for the teeth of the children, a two-hour dental appointment is filled each week by those taking their turn.

Among the most active and loyal members of the congregation of the Rolling Plains Methodist Church are the young people of the Avondale Children's Home. The older boys lend their aid to the church ushers and the girls find their dining room experience at the home makes them popular helpers when the church women serve meals.

Preparatory to church membership older children from the "big family" attend the Saturday morning confirmation class conducted by the church minister, the Rev. John E. Zinsmeister. This year the group of seven from the home consists of Jim Shipman, Tom Billingsley, Larry Stainbrook, Terry Quarterman, Linda Pride, Velma Ihinger, and Bessie Wineman.

On March 25 and 26 the Rolling Plains Church will be sponsoring a minstrel with a cast of 70 in the Newton School. The talents of several of the children of the home will make a definite contribution to the production. Before a backdrop painted by "sister" Ginny Corbin 10 girls of the Avondale family will sing and dance. One of their "brothers" will be programmed in a song and dance routine.

The 4-H Club and Boy and Girl Scout troops of the neighborhood afford the children of the home opportunities for training and experience especially designed for their age group.

As the young residents of the home express a desire and show willingness to continue with advanced education "father" and "mother" Caughey ally themselves and assume the role of friends and reassuring counselors. From the "biggest family" one young man has successfully financed himself through Ohio University and is now teaching at Roseville High School. One girl after completing office training at Bliss Business College is now employed in Columbus. With the assistance of the Business and Professional Women's Club 'nurses' training at Bethesda Hospital prepared one of the Avondale girls for her present position at White Cross Hospital in Columbus.

Before Mr. and Mrs. Caughey became administrators of the Avondale home 11 years ago Aug. 1, Mr. Caughey was for 25 years packing room foreman at Hazel-Atlas Glass Plant No. 1. Mrs. Caughey's previous years had been spent as a housewife and mother of their two sons. Dick, whose wife is the former Sue Kendall, lives in Columbus and Jack, Jr., and his wife, the former Jean Hunt, live on Newark road.

—Gatewood Studio

Their Wedding Portrait

MR. and MRS. CHARLES E. STRICKLER
(Beulah Mae Kinder)

Double ring rites were read Sunday, June 4, for Miss Beulah Mae Kinder and Charles Edward Strickler, son of Mr. and Mrs. Charles Strickler of Avondale. The former Miss Kinder, ward of Mr. and Mrs. John S. Caughey of South Zanesville, Route 2, is a graduate of Roseville High School. Both Mr. and Mrs. Strickler are members of the Rolling Plains Methodist Church. Mr. Strickler, also a graduate of Roseville High School, is an aviation machinist's mate, 3rd class, with the U. S. Navy. The couple will live in Patuxent River, Md.

"They have been wonderful years. We have had a few heartaches, but mostly happiness. We heard from most of the children who have left us and it pleases us to know that the majority of them are doing quite well. In all, our life has been very full and gratifying."

Mrs. John S. Caughey, matron at Avondale from 1949 to 1962.

Left
Newspaper clipping, June 11, 1961.

"[Pops] Caughey was such a sweet man. He worked hard for us."

Beulah Kinder-Strickler
(Pops Caughey gave Beulah away at her wedding to Charles).

Opposite Page
Newspaper article titled "Muskingum County's 'Biggest Family' Consists of 53 Children," March 20, 1960.

"We both liked going to Lake Isabella, Grange and American Legion dances; football games were exciting."

Jackie Vandenbark-Jones, Beulah Kinder-Strickler

Roger Russell, summer recreational director, accompanies Avondale Home children on bicycle trip.

Jam-Packed Recreation Program

Summer Is Action Time For Avondale Children

Story and Pictures
By DERON MIKAL

The Avondale Children's Home employed a summer recreational director three years ago and since that time youngsters there have enjoyed a jam-packed program.

Roger Russell of Fultonham, a social studies teacher at Maysville High School and reserve basketball coach there, has spent his second summer at the Children's Home as recreational director. His interest in the youngsters coupled with his professional training in physical education make him an ideal choice for the job.

THE YOUNGSTERS, 24 of whom are of school age—have gone swimming regularly at Lake Isabella in East Fultonham, hiked through woods and stripmined areas, fished in farm ponds and local streams, rode horses and a mule at the home and bicycled sometimes as far as 10 or 13 miles.

They also took advantage of their own playground equipment, swings, slides, monkey bars, basketball court, baseball and softball diamond and a seven-hole golf course they constructed themselves this summer.

They also made walking stilts from scrap lumber.

THEY HAVE attended many special events including the Muskingum County Fair, the Soap Box Derby, Shrine basketball game, Phlin Firemen's Festival, and being Fourth - of - July guests of Maple Drive - In where they were treated with food, soft drinks and popcorn.

Dale Tysinger treats the youngsters to movies at the Liberty or State theater about once a week, and they have an

Monty Hanning tries out the playground slide.

Girl is put astride the home's mule for her first ride.

Monkey bars give school-age children opportunity to develop muscles.

Youngsters try their skill on seven-hole golf course they constructed.

Children try out stilts they made themselves.

open invitation at the Sky-Way. Recently the boys were given tickets by the president of the Cleveland Indians to see a baseball game at Cleveland Stadium. They watched as the Indians beat the Yankees.

They went to Old Man's Cave recently, had an all - day picnic at Cutler Lake, and the boys were treated to an overnight camping trip on the Fred Curry farm near Fultonham where they caught 90 to 100 fish in a farm pond. Some of the fish were cleaned and fried for breakfast the following morning by Russell.

A wiener roast at the home will cap the summer's events just before Russell returns to teaching.

IN THE EVENING youngsters play badminton, croquet, billiards and checkers, hear records and watch television. Bargain City gives the Home several large supplies of candy

Tim Church and Dick Dietenbech engage in boy talk.

each year, and each youngster is given a treat as he or she settles down to watch television. Mrs. Anna Caughey is the administrator, and she is assisted by two housemothers, two cooks, two laundresses, and a maintenance man.

Pony rides are enjoyed by children of all ages.

Hike through Muskingum County hills is led by Russell.

Flag in front of home is lowered at sunset.

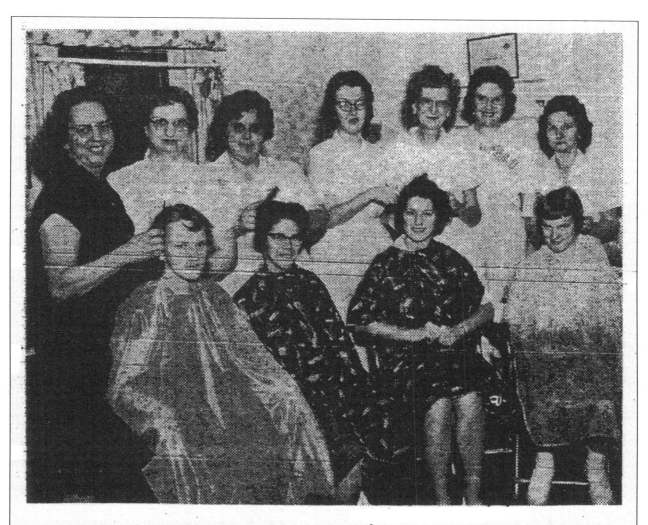

Twenty-six girls at Avondale Children's Home received permanents for Christmas as gifts from members of the Hairdressers Guild. Four of the youngsters shown here are, from left, Velma Ihinger, Rita Boyd, Pat Novaria and Sandra Harris. Members of the Guild, shown standing from left are. Miss Fae Wooley, Mrs. Samuel Carrell, Miss Francina Thomas, Miss Phyllis

Above
Newspaper clipping from the *Times Recorder*, December 10, 1961.

Opposite Page
Newspaper clipping from the *Times Recorder*, August 27, 1967.

Above
Newspaper clipping, December 9, 1961.

Right
One can only imagine the commotion caused at the home when lightning struck the kitchen area causing injuries to two staff members and a resident as well as hundreds of dollars worth of damages. Only one of the two large chimneys remains standing today.

"I did not like it much that our prom dresses were recycled and pretty worn out."

Beulah Kinder-Strickler

Miss Emma West, left, and Mrs. Marggaret Adams, both cooks at the Children's Home at Avondale, survey the damage in the kitchen of the Home after lightning struck both chimneys during Friday's brief thunderstorm. In photo at right, Alva Hittle, county maintenance superintendent, appraises the damage to the chimneys and roof of the Home. County commissioners will meet this morning with an insurance adjuster and building contractors to arrange for immediate repairs.

GIRL INJURED

Lightning Strikes Children's Home

Twin bolts of lightning, only seconds apart, split both brick chimneys at the Muskingum County Children's Home at Avondale during the brief thunderstorm at 4:30 p.m. Friday.

The lightning followed the chimneys to the kitchen and boiler room, causing several hundred dollars damage, ruining the vent hood over the stove, splitting the roof over the boiler room and showering bricks and debris over equipment in both rooms.

Three women employes and a girl at the home were in the kitchen when it was struck. Barbara Bailey, 15, received a cut finger and was treated at a physician's office. There were no other injuries. Also in the kitchen were Mrs. Margaret Adams and Miss Emma West, both cooks, and Miss Eva Hagley, housekeeper.

Hutson Barnes, president of the county commissioners, said that the county maintenance crew, under Superintendent Alva Hittle, was setting up a temporary kitchen in the old school building back of the home and making emergency repairs.

The commissioners are to meet at 9 a.m. today at the home with two contractors and an insurance adjuster to arrange for immediate repairs to the building.

The brief storm dumped .21 of an inch of rain on the area in 20 minutes, starting about 4:30 p.m., according to the weather station at Municipal Airport.

Temperatures dropped from 80 degrees at 4 p.m. to 68 at 5 o'clock. The day's high reading was 85 at 2 p.m.

A glider, piloted by Dean Svec, 38, of Bedford, landed at 4:15 p.m. on a field owned by John Gibson about a mile south of New Concord just west of Ohio 76.

The Ohio Highway Patrol said Svec landed the glider due to the approaching storm. Svec was en route from Richland, Ind., where he had left at 11:15 a.m., to Morristown, in Belmont County. There was no damage to the glider or the field and the pilot was not injured.

The patrol said a car with a trailer was to have picked up the glider at Morristown but was forced to come back to New Concord where the glider was loaded and returned to Richland.

Historic Bell That Once Rang In Statehouse Here Located

Display Of Relic Seen

By DAVID SHINN

An historic old bell which hung in the old Statehouse and Courthouse from 1814 to 1874 now lies amid a pile of junk in the Courthouse basement.

Time may bring happier days for the old relic, however. The county commissioners have told county maintenance men to prepare a framework to hold the bell so it can be put on permanent display in the first floor Courthouse corridor.

It is expected the work will not be done until sometime next winter because the maintenance men have a heavy summer schedule keeping the various county buildings in proper repair, the commissioners said. The bell will have to be thoroughly cleaned before it can be properly displayed.

Meantime, the maintenance men work on cleaning the bell whenever they have time between their other jobs.

The bell was nearly hauled to a junk yard a few years ago, but at the last minute the late Jack Caughey, superintendent of Avondale Children's Home asked that he be allowed to take the bell to the children's home. County commissioners permitted him to do so. There the bell stayed until it was moved back to the Courthouse about three years ago.

Story continues at far right...

Walter Bugglin of the county maintenance department is shown cleaning the historic old bell which hung in the old Statehouse and Courthouse from 1814 to 1874. Plans have been made to display the bell in the Courthouse. The bell is now in the Courthouse basement.

Left
Newspaper clipping from the *Times Recorder*, June 12, 1964.

Continued from clipping at left.

The bell was once thought lost, but in 1934 someone found it hanging in the old Fourth street tower at the Courthouse. It was taken down and was made one of the highlights of the Zanesville homecoming celebration in August of that year.

Zanesville Presbyterians bought the bell, the first in Zanesville, in 1814. They worshiped in homes, barns and the Senate chamber of the old Statehouse, then used by the county. Many of the church members lived across the river in Putnam in those days and few persons in those days owned clocks or watches.

The Presbyterians raised $400 toward purchase of a bell. The county commissioners also made an appropriation.

The bell was ordered from Thomas W. Devering foundry in Philadelphia, where the Liberty Bell, made in England in 1752, was twice recast.

The new bell came by boat down the Ohio and up the Muskingum. From the keelboat it was hauled by wagon to the front of the Courthouse at Main and Fourth streets. With hangings, it weighed 675 pounds.

Hanging in the old Courthouse until 1874, the bell became a part of the city's history. For instance, it rang to announce the firing on Fort Sumter which marked the beginning of the Civil War.

The bell was tolled for funerals to designate the cause and progress of the procession. The ringing always wound up with three quick strokes as the bier reached the grave. At every corner or change of pallbearers the bell rang once.

Each day, the bell was rung

Story continues on next page...

Left
Jack and Jill Dutcher examine bell that was hung in Courthouse in 1814 and now, saved from the junk yard, stands near back door of Avondale Children's Home. Picture dated November 5, 1961.

Right Top
Newspaper clipping reporting John Caughey's death, Feb. 22, 1964.

Right Bottom
Avondale budget, 1971. Please treat yourself to the narrative below the budget line items. It is absolutely hysterical.

Opposite Page
Article from *Times Recorder*, September 6, 1970.

Continued from clipping on the previous page.

at certain times to announce the hour. It also was rung, at a rapid pace, to announce fires. When that happened, residents would rush into the streets with buckets and a bucket brigade was quickly formed. It was also used to summon school children to classes, and to call worshipers to church on Sundays.

Some amusing incidents are part of the bell's history. One night a man known as Davy Ayers climbed into the Courthouse tower and wound rags around the clapper until the ball was as large as his head. Next morning, there was no 8 a.m. bell. The ringer told the mayor the bell was cracked he couldn't make it ring. Worry was seen on many faces that day. However, in the afternoon a check was made and the trick discovered. In the meantime, a large number of theories had been advanced to account for the supposed damage.

The old bell tolled for the funeral of Zanesville's founder, John McIntire, who died July 29, 1815, at the age of 56.

When the present Courthouse was completed in 1877, the bell was placed in the Fourth street tower. Eventually, that tower showed signs of falling and was removed. The bell was then stored for many years in a basement room

Note
The historic bell can now be viewed in the Muskingum County Courthouse lobby.

FOLLOWING OPERATION

Jack Caughey, Children's Home Superintendent, Dies

JACK CAUGHEY

John (Jack) Caughey Sr., 60, superintendent of Avondale Children's Home since 1950, died unexpectedly about 6:50 p.m. Friday in Waterman Memorial Hospital at Eustis, Fla. He underwent an emergency operation for a ruptured ulcer Thursday at the hospital.

Mr. Caughey and his wife, Sarah Shiplett Caughey, had been in Florida vacationing since Feb. 2.

Mr. Caughey was born in Pennsylvania, a son of Mr. and Mrs. John Stevens and Daisy Maude Caughey. He formerly served in the Navy. His parents moved to a farm near White Cottage while he was in the Navy, and when he was discharged a short time later, he became a resident of this area. He lived on farms most of his life. Mr. Caughey was a familiar figure in this area.

Surviving are two sons John Jr. of Newark road, and Richard of Athens; and an adopted son, Wayne Rambo of Newark road.

In 1962, the Caughey family was chosen to represent the Zanesville district of the Ohio Methodist Conference as the Methodist Family of the year. Mr. Caughey was a member of Rolling Plains Methodist Church.

Mr. and Mrs. James Way have been supervising operations at the orphanage in the absence of Mr. and Mrs. Caughey and are expected to continue to do so until a replacement can be appointed by county commissioners. There are 50 children at the home at present.

Avondale Children's Home

Budget 1971

Superintendent		$ 4,500.00
Employees		23,100.00
9-B-15	supplies	12,000.00
9-B-16	new equipment	1,000.00
9-B-17	repairs	2,500.00
9-B-18	contracts service	7,000.00
9-B-21	all other	5,000.00

The raise for Superintendent is $222.00 per year.

The raise for employees is $20.00 raise for each employee per month.

Also $250.00 per month for another staff member. When Mr. Porter talked the staff into doubling up on their work, he said he would divide the salary among them. This never materialized, so our staff has to work many hours during vacations.

The big raise in 9-B-18 is because I have had to transfer the last 3 months from other codes. The gas, electric telephone and doctor and dentist comes under 9-B-18. I'm sure you must know this.

submitted by (Mrs.) Anna Caughey
Superintendent
Avondale Children's Home

Avondale Children Learn Someone Really Cares

'Big Brothers' Make Days Little Brighter

By ERIC LAND

Most children growing up in normal homes enjoy and never forget their childhood with "big brothers and big sisters" to look to for understanding, fun, and even a punch in the nose. But youngsters at the Avondale Children's home have little opportunity to share with other family members the joys of growing up with a pair of parents who care and understand the problems a youngster might have preying on his mind.

Most of the children at the home are from broken homes. Years ago, there were at one time nearly 60 living at the home. Presently there are 34, but those 34 need the guidance, love and the "being there" feeling parents c a n give in a normal home.

MOST OF THE children say they like the home. And why not? There's a warm bed at night, and food to eat, the necessities of life. And there's a dedicated home staff to look after their daily needs. But at a crucial time in a child's life, while he is growing, acquiring knowledge of life around him, that's a time when more than food and bedding means existence. It's when each individual child craves a personal companionship, a friend, someone to look up to and to learn from. And there is one girl we know of who comes to know her own self much more important, here.

She is Miss Kay Dalton, 21, of 705½ Monwood avenue. Kay teaches first grade at the Newton school, and during the school year she is in close contact with the children from the home as they attend there too. Kay is studying elementary education at Ohio University Zanesville, and worked this past summer with the Muskingum County Children's services. Her office was located at 4th Woodlawn avenue.

She started the summer as a case worker's aide. Her original assignment was to be with the children at the home one day a week, but as the summer progressed, Kay could be found at Avondale three times, and sometimes more, a week.

KAY, LIKE many other interested citizens, feels that the idea of a big brother or big sister program, appeals to the youngsters.

"They will be our future citizens," she said making Zanesville into whatever it will be. All the children need is a little help and understanding.

Kay feels that if someone would take the children on family outings, "only one or two hours a week," the youngsters would begin to understand family living, and how to adjust.

This past summer, Miss Dalton took the children to numerous community events, ranging from roller skating to the county fair. The OUZ summer players trekked to the home to put on one of their plays.

One event Kay will fondly never forget, was a humble bike-hike to Roseville. Three hike-outs of hike time occurred but Miss Dalton and nine little girls made the trip.

CHILDREN at the home — they range from 4 to 18 years of age — are awake by 7:30 a.m. After breakfast, the smaller youngsters go outside and play, weather permitting, while the older ones assist in the kitchen, scrubbing floors and other menial tasks.

Roger Russell, 23, a teacher at Maysville High School, works part-time at the home, and can usually be found with the boys. Some of the children have been to the Cleveland Indians day baseball; others have visited old Man's Cave. They camp and swim often, and have also visited Buckeye Lake, played golf, and seen most of the general matinee movies at the two Zanesville theaters.

According to the matron, Mrs. Dorah Coughey, the Children's Home is turning into more of just a "receiving home," where children live for a year or less, until they can be placed in foster homes. Mrs. Coughey said that years ago, children grew up, and not in on a road, nearly 8 but from the floor. All the children could see it.

"At one time," she said, ...

The housemother, then took the dog the girl had asked for, and put in on a nail, on the said ever since. Mrs. W a t t s, one of the ... but no one was allowed to take it off the nail. The little animal has been ... housemothers, said, "They get everything they want, in it belongs to them." When asked about the dog ...

RUSSELL said that the children wind up doing more than average youngster, but "they need so much more." Some are preoccupied with problems at their homes. Some have been rejected at their home and now they're trying to make the best of it.

MANY times, discipline is strict. Miss Dalton took 11 children from the home one day in mid-summer to attend the St. Nicholas festival. Stuffed animals were donated to all the little ones, along with bats and various other prizes. One of the girls, had her eye on a bear puppy, and asked especially for it. Miss Dalton, attempting to teach the child that she should be happy with whatever she receives, especially when someone is making a donation, gave the girl a red dog on purpose. When they returned to the home, the little girl ran to one of the housemothers and told her what had happened.

... and most of the children belonged to 4-H and other clubs.

There are many things lacking at the Avondale Children's home. Probably, the most important would be to know that someone really cares.

"Big Sister" Kay Dalton romps with a number of her charges on the well-kept grounds at the Avondale Children's Home.

Children spend a lot of time sitting down at a recent roller-skating party but Miss Dalton, right, always had a word of encouragement for each.

Roger Russell adjusts equipment of young football enthusiast.

Miss Dalton joins children for a ride at St. Nicholas festival.

At times action was fast and furious at skating party.

99

Mrs. Caughey Resigns

Roger Russell Appointed Children's Home Director

Roger Russell, newly - appointed director of the Avondale Children's Home, poses on the lawn in front of the brick structure located on the Roseville road. He replaces Mrs. Anna Caughey who served as matron of the home for 20 years, and who recently resigned.

Roger Russell, 32, who has served as recreational director for the Avondale Children's Home for the past six summers, has been appointed director of the home effective Sept. 1, it was announced by William Geyer, chairman of the Children's Services Board. He will replace Mrs. Anna Caughey, who has been in charge of the home for 20 years and who recently resigned

The job pays $6,000 per year and also provides living quarters for Russell and his family in an apartment in back of the home. His wife, who will act as his assistant, will receive $2,400 per year.

Russell is a native of Fultonham and graduated from Roseville High School. He graduated from Muskingum College in 1962 with a B.S. degree in health and physical education. He played two years of college basketball, one year of football.

He started teaching school at Newton Elementary school in 1959, finishing his college education in a catch - as - catch can manner, using all his ingenuity to gather credits where he could. During one hectic summer he was driving to Ohio State for one course he could get nowhere else, then racing pell - mell to New Concord the same day for a course at Muskingum College. He took a few of his required courses from Ohio University - Zanesville and even acquired one from a correspondence school.

He was at Newton five years, teaching the seventh and eighth grades and spending two years as physical education instructor. He went from Newton to Roseville High School where he was head basketball coach for three years and assisted in coaching football and track. For the past four years he has been a teacher at Maysville High School and will continue to teach morning courses there in government.

Russell will be in charge of a staff consisting of two house mothers, one relief house mother, two cooks and a laundress. All live in at the home except the laundress

He is married to the former Linda Shields of Roseville and has three daughters, Christy, 12; Cindy, 10 and Cathy, 5 years old.

Above
Lawn behind the boys wing and laundry building.

Left
Roger Russell shooting pool on the boys' side.

Opposite Page
Newspaper clipping from August 28, 1971.

Below
This Avondale vehicle made many trips to Lake Isabella and other public outings in the early 1970s.

AVONDALE HOME

Above
Roger Russell shown above as a teacher in the Maysville School District.

Above
Roger Russel visiting Avondale in 2011.

Right Top
Avondale boys prepping their Soap Box Derby cars for the big race.

Right Middle
Roger Russel loading up Soap Box Derby cars for transport to McIntire Avenue.

Right Bottom
Soap Box Derby race. The car on the right is being driven by an Avondale boy.

Left
Roger Russell and several youth on horseback. This is one of the few known pictures of the old barn, which burned down in 1973.

Below Left
A typical day at Roger Russell's Avondale.

Below
Newspaper ad, September, 1970.

Right
Newspaper feature wishing "Good Luck," to Soap Box Derby entrants, Danny Woerner and Richard McPherson, July 11, 1971.

Below Right
Soap Box Derby day in the pit area.

Below
Newspaper ad, September, 1970.

DANNY WOERNER   RICHARD McPHERSON

Foster Home Group Formed Here

April 1, 1971

Last year 487 Muskingum County children were taken from homes in which they were being under-nourished, mistreated or were unwanted, and placed in foster homes, Avondale Children's Home, or adoptive homes, through the efforts of Children's Services.

Many of these children are currently being cared for in 62 homes in Muskingum County. Foster parents receive $55 per month for each child under five years old and $65 per month for each one over that age.

More foster homes are needed and a group has been formed called Friends of Children's Services, to assist in seeing that neglected or abused youngsters are exposed to happy, healthful environments and learn the meaning of giving and receiving love and care.

Mrs. Melvin Krohn, of 522 East Highland drive, is chairman of the group and is appealing now for used clothing of all types, infant through teen-age sizes, to help foster parents keep these children well-clothed.

In addition, Mrs. Donna Schafer, executive secretary of Children's Services, has announced the creation of a speaker's bureau to acquaint interested social, civic and church groups with its work and to enlist their help in alleviating the hardships sometimes imposed on helpless youngsters.

Interested groups may contact Mrs. Schaefer at Children's Services, 440 Woodlawn avenue, or Mrs. Charles Moeser at 724 Fairmont avenue.

Above
Newspaper clipping, April 1, 1971.

Left
Paintings that used to hang in the dining room for many years.

Above
Newspaper ad, September, 1970.

105

Firemen from four fire departments battled a fire early Wednesday evening which destroyed the livestock barn at Avondale Childrens Home. None of the animals housed in the two - story structure was injured. The blaze apparently started in a hay mow. (Photo by J. Frank Jaworowski)

Avondale Barn Burns

By DERON MIKAL
TR Staff Reporter

The livestock barn at Avondale Childrens Home was destroyed by fire early Wednesday evening, shaking the hopes and dreams of 30 boys and girls at the home.

Roger Russell, director of the home said "the life - line of activity for the children is gone now. All the boys and girls had something to do at the barn caring for and feeding the animals."

However, none of the 16 ponies, five calves, a mule and a goat was hurt in the blaze that started about 6:15 p.m. and whipped out of control in minutes.

Russell himself shooed calves from the barn to safety and grabbed saddles, bridles, harnesses and accessories from the barn, tossing them to children waiting in safe range from the structure.

Firemen from South Zanesville, Newton Township Volunteer Fire Department, Roseville and Crooksville were on the scene to fight the blaze. The fire may have started because of combustion from molded hay, Russell said. Some 300 bales were stored in the mow.

Most of the barn was destroyed despite the two-hour battle to save the structure.

It was 11 - year - old Tim Haser who discovered the blaze while on his way to feed the calves. The calves were going to be sold as feeders to buy saddles, Russell said.

"Our animal program at the home has given children here a new outlook on life. Their own problems seem minimal compared to the day - to - day needs of the livestock. There is also the pleasure they get in riding and showing their ponies. That's important," Russell said.

The ponies and livestock were donated by a number of persons in the area who wanted to contribute to the welfare of the children through the animal program.

Muskingum County commissioners were at the scene accessing the damage. Commissioner Scott Patton said the building was covered by insurance.

A bus barn, garage and some livestock loafing sheds were saved by firemen. A farm tractor, garden tractor and some bicycles were stored in other buildings and escaped damage. All the buildings were attached at the roof line, Russell reported.

Night of the Fire: April 11, 1973

The night of the barn fire at the Avondale Children's home was a very traumatic time for the children and the staff. We watched as the barn erupted into flames and knew there was not much we could do. The wooden barn filled with hay and combustible materials was soon consumed. We had a boy, at that time, that was a suspected of setting previous fires before he came to live with us. The cause of those fires was never proved as neither was the Avondale fire. He did happen to be on kitchen duty, that night, which would have given him access to the scene.

When the fire was first noticed, the fire department was called and I ran to the barn but it was too far gone to have any chance of putting it out. The fire was mainly in the hay loft at that time. Not thinking of the danger, I simply reacted. Thinking only of the horse equipment we had all worked so hard to get and how much the kids enjoyed the horses, I ran into the barn and drug out all the saddles and equipment I could get in one trip since that one trip was all that I would be able to make. I do remember the sparks falling around me as I made my quick trip in the tractor opening to the barn where the horse equipment was kept.

I really felt bad for the kids and their loss but it all worked out. No animals were lost as they were in the pasture. No one was hurt! We got a new pole barn and the life resumed, pretty much as before. The twenty horses and ponies and twenty-seven kids and staff hardly noticed the change ….just a slight inconvenience for a short period of time.

– by Roger Russell, Avondale Superintendent 1971-1974

"I have good memories of Avondale!"

Rose Oliver – 1974
(Rose has shared her time, talent, and treasure working with children at the Muskingum County Juvenile Court for 20+ years).

Opposite Page
Newspaper article, April 12, 1973.

Horse Given To Home

They say, "Don't look a gift horse in the mouth." But Charlie wouldn't mind. He is the horse given to the Avondale Children's Home by Julie Hill, daughter of Dr. and Mrs. William Hill of 3325 North Willow drive. Charlie was a two - place winner at the 1970 Muskingum County Fair. The family could not care for the pony, Roger Russell, recreational director at the home, said

he has been urging gifts of farm animals for the Children's Home to give the youngsters an outside interest. All the children have adopted "Charlie" as their own already, Russell said. Shown with the prize-winning pony are (left to right) Teresa Glosser, former owner Julie Hill, Esther Johnson and George Snodgrass (on the horse), and Richard McPherson.

Left
Roger the calf. Guess who he was named after!

Opposite Page
Newspaper clipping, March 5, 1971.

Below
Newspaper clipping, December 2, 1973.

Greg Shumate, 15 (left) and Rick Tyo, 14, help keep up maintenance on quarters in preparation for Open House scheduled next Sunday.

Avondale Children's Home Director Roger Russell referees basketball game for boys during evening recreation in hall converted from school rooms into recreational uses. Shown participating in the game are Mike Stevens, 13 (left) and Jack Roden, 13.

Avondale Children's Home Open House Is Next Sunday

Above & Right
Newspaper article, December 2, 1973.

Above
Melissa the donkey, one of the many pets of the Roger Russell era.

Above
Mike, the goat, Yeller, the lab, and Speckles, the basset/beagle mix. Mike, the goat, wandered the property and even found his way into the kitchen on one occasion.

Avondale Children's Home will hold Open House from 1 to 4 p.m. Sunday, Dec. 9, it was announced by Home Director Roger Russell.

Open House is scheduled partly so taxpayers can see how their money is being spent in the care of Muskingum County foster children placed at the home and partly to encourage greater participation from the community in activities at the home, Russell said.

Tours will be conducted throughout the facility by select youngsters at the Children's Home. Living quarters, dining facilities, dormitories and recreation halls will be emphasized on the tour.

Children's Homes have been historically considered ominous and strange to onlookers who view youngsters in custody as orphaned waifs subjected to who knows what. Many early English novels are built around just such a plot-line.

To help educate against that notion, an Open House will give the general public a first-hand view of the Children's Home and what it is accomplishing now under the supervision of Roger Russell and his wife, Linda.

The Russells live in an apartment within the facilities along with their three children. They are there around the clock. The institutional feeling that can develop easily in such a facility is minimized tremendously as the family pursues its own life-style there.

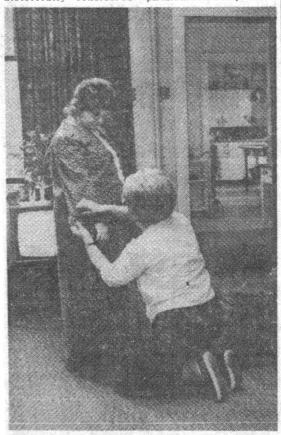

Mrs. Eleanor Watts, Children's Home cook, pitches in to help sew dress for Kaye Moody, 15, of the home who will help conduct tours for Open House.

110

Share Life-Style

They mix freely and easily among the youngsters, sharing meals at times, joining in recreational activities, and getting to community events with the children.

Russell has been a grade and high school teacher most of his adult life, teaching at Newton and Roseville and he is presently on the teaching staff of Maysville High School until noon each day.

He became interested in the Avondale Children's Home when he served during summers as Recreational Director. At that time he took youngsters swimming, on trail hikes, to community gatherings, and had them come together in group sports playing soft ball, badminton, baseball and yard games along with bicycling and horseback riding.

In fact, the home now cares for over 20 ponies, many of

Photos by Marjorie Trost

which are given over to the care of one of the youngsters whose personal problems diminish in an eager attempt to make the animal comfortable and loved.

Barn Rebuilt

Only last year, the large barn that housed the animals was destroyed by fire and a new one is presently being built and should be under roof before bad weather sets in. There is enough acreage on the Avondale Children's Home farm to support the animals and local farmers in the area have done their part in contributing oats and corn for the upkeep of the ponies.

Bill Dawson of near Roseville was instrumental in getting many of the ponies transported to the farm and is still active in seeing after their care and welfare.

So, in fact, we are talking about having youngsters participate in a rural setting, going to the barn, feeding and graining the animals, having pet goats, dogs, cats, ducks, calves, donkeys, fish, hamsters and enjoying time spent with

the farm collective. Older boys and girls help put the hay in and help with some of the larger farm chores.

Inside, they share their time with housemothers who are there 24 hours a day on split shifts, mending, sewing, playing games, watching television with the youngsters and providing a home atmosphere as much as humanly possible.

Started 62 Years Ago

It all started 62 years ago this month when the structure was built at a cost of $19,356 by E. Mast, providing for a structure capable of caring for 50 children. Most foster children in Muskingum County were sent to the Tuscarawas County Children's Home at Canal Dover then.

Thanks to the Times Recorder Christmas Fund and the generous support of hundreds in the community over the years, money is made available for recreational projects and a huge Christmas for the boys and girls at the home over the holidays.

Above
Modes of transportation at the Avondale Children's Home has ranged from walking, biking, horseback riding, car, truck, van, bus and tractor.

Left
Continuation of newspaper article, December 2, 1973.

Boys' lounge has living room comfort and makes homework pleasant at Avondale Children's Home. Shown (left to right) are Mike Rush, 15, Tom McPherson, 13, and George Snodgrass, 14. House mothers often share the living room with the boys and are available to help with homework, games and keep conversation going.

Avondale 'Mom' Has A 'Way' With Kids

By JOHN RAY
TR Staff Writer

Mrs. Mildred Way is a warm, matronly woman who obviously instills instant trust and confidence in children entrusted to her care.

Now supervisor of house parents at Avondale Children's Home, she has retired from employment at the home three times over the years but has been irresistibly drawn back by her love of children.

She was born and raised on a ranch in Nebraska and after she married Jim Way, the couple lived on a ranch in Wyoming.

Jim Stayed On

Later he became a construction worker and came to White Cottage when the Tertling Bros. Construction Company started the coal strip mining operation at Avondale. Jim stayed on with the strip mining operation as master mechanic after Tertling's job was completed.

In 1953 the couple's son, Jim Jr., was a junior student at Marietta College. He was returning to Marietta following a visit home and riding with a group of other students.

It was extremely foggy and suddenly, at the crest of a hill, a truck loomed out of the mists, too close to avoid. The car Jim Jr. was riding in crashed into its rear end, killing him and another youth.

Job To Job

Following the son's death Jim Way went back to the construction trade, traveling from job to job, taking Mildred with him. The two lived in a trailer, towed by their car, but still retained possession of their house in White Cottage. It was difficult for them to adjust to the fact that their athletic and popular son was gone.

The Ways came back to White Cottage in 1958. They attended Rolling Plains United

Twelve-year-old Jay Shuttles (center) and Bobby Cannon, 12, share a book and a laugh with Mrs. Mildred Way who has long been recognized for her sincere love and caring for the children at the Avondale Children's Home.

"I had to teach myself to shoot pool," she recalled. "One day I invited a new youngster to play."

First Woman

"Mrs. Way, you're the first woman I ever played pool with," he said.

"Didn't your mother ever play pool with you?"

"No, she was a Christian," he said.

A new, black boy said to her, right at the outset, "I might as well tell you I'm prejudiced against whites."

Mrs. Way "retired" in 1963, but the children needed her so eight days later she was back at work. In June, 1973, she retired again but was back again from April to October, 1974, when she retired for the third time. She came back last June 3 to accept the interim appointment of director, which she held until this past October, when Charles Jones was appointed.

Activities Vary

The kids enjoy a lot of activities, including occasional dances, bingo games, bowling and parties. An activity coordinator organizes the events.

The money donated each year to the Avondale Children's Home Christmas fund is used partly for Christmas gifts, but some of it is held back for later use. This permits such activities as visits to big league baseball games, camping trips or skating parties.

Last year two new tents were bought and the money is also used for special things for school, such as class rings. The money bought a guitar for one girl and pays her transportation to and from her teacher, who gives her free lessons.

Home For Christmas

"All the children who want to can spend a few days at home for Christmas," Mrs. Way explained. "Then when they all come back we have a big Christmas party. That way even those who didn't get a present at home get one here. They are all permitted to make up a Christmas list of things they'd like to have. This year one of the boys who used to live here is going to bring his band to entertain at our party," she said.

"The rewards of this job are recognized when you can look around you and see what you have accomplished. Most of our kids came from unfortunate backgrounds but have done well in spite of that. They have benefitted by being here.

"Mr. Jones is an excellent counselor. He is teaching the children to improve their own images, to have more faith and confidence in themselves. I expect a big improvement here."

Kids Don't Forget

Mrs. Way regularly hears from a former ward — a black youth — who is now a successful Navy career man. Another grateful youth is a junior at Marietta College — the older brother of a boy now at the home — who writes her often.

With that kind of return on her investment, how can Mrs. Way ever retire with any degree of finality? The magnetism works both ways — she loves the kids and they love her.

Above
Typical scene behind the boys' wing.

Opposite Page
Newspaper clipping from the *Times Recorder*, December 11, 1977.
Ms. Way had an impact on Avondale that can't be described. She is always the first person mentioned by anyone involved with Avondale during her many years. She was a true original and loved by all. Avondale would be much different today if it were not for Mildred Way.

Avondale Improvements Replaces Darkened Past

By NANCY KEELEY
Assistant News Editor

"Discipline is a good thing. As long as you know the rules, you can follow them," a teenage boy leaned forward in his chair at Avondale Youth Center and tired to describe life there.

"I think I've been helped here. The rules aren't like the ones you have at home. Parents have rules too, but it just isn't the same," he struggled to define the difference and finally shrugged. "It's just different."

"Avondale is a place kids should be sent to straighten out. It isn't a place where a kid should spend his life," a girl commented. Sunlight brightened the small lounge and a volleyball game was in progress in the front yard.

This time last year Avondale Youth Center, formerly Avondale Children's Home, had been a county trouble spot. Schools recorded a high rate of truancy, students grades were low and attitudes poor. Runaway rates were high.

Reputations of the center and its residents suffered.

Sgt. Robert Stephenson, juvenile officer for the Muskingum County Sheriff's Department, doesn't see the children in the home much any more. It's not because he doesn't want to, but because he's not needed as often professionally.

"Things are very much improved," he assessed. "We're not getting the runaways and the kids are doing well.

"Besides that there are 24 children. When we had all the trouble there were only about 15. The attitudes of the kids have changed. They're less hostile," Stephenson added.

"They know they are wanted and someone really does care. Avondale's staff is doing a fine job," he said.

"They've remodeled," Stephenson continued, "and that has something to do with it. The kids are happier. They treat me as a human being as well as a police officer. Most of the change has taken place in the past two or three months," he said.

Candy Sharp, left, Susie Anderson, center, and Kathy Largo join forces to prepare for the ninth grade graduation dance in Maysville Local School District. One of the things that have made life brighter at Avondale is remodeling of the residents' rooms by Muskingum County commissioners. (Photo by Brian Dutro)

"I think the most important part is people are showing them love and attention," Stephenson concluded.

Director Praised

"Things are a lot better and the kids seem better adjusted," said Muskingum County Sheriff Bernie Gibson.

"Charlie (Charles Jones, director of Avondale) is the biggest thing that's happened down there. He has done more in a different way. We also worked it out with the Muskingum County commissioners to do some remodeling," Gibson explained.

Muskingum County Commissioners recently spent over $7,000 for improvements at Avondale. Work included lowered ceilings, repainting, curtains, carpeting, furniture, tiling and restroom remodeling.

"We tried to make each room a little different and bought captain's beds for storage so the kids could have a little privacy," Commissioner William Embree said.

"We did the remodeling to improve the building, but most importantly to show the kids we have respect for them. There is no incentive to keep rooms clean, if they are in terrible shape in the beginning," he added.

"Charlie is consistant," Gibson said. He has levels the kids work through and he doesn't play favorites. He's professional and he insists the staff be the same."

"Before Jones was named director, the runaway rate averaged one a week. There have been three in the past three or four months and one of them was a child who had been placed in the home that day,"

"Before Jones was named director, the runaway rate averaged one a week. There have been three in the past three or four months and one of them was a child who had been placed in the home that day," Gibson related.

Grades Improve

Dennis Hales, principal at Maysville Junior High School, also has noticed a vast change. "All of their grades have gone up," he observed. "I can think of no negative changes and the kids are happier.

"When you think these children are referred from juvenile detention centers and courts and already have more than enough problems, they have come a long way. I'm impressed."

When Charles Jones came to Avondale last November, he initiated a contract between residents in the home. It is a list of goals to be reached in relationships with others, impulse control and self-esteem.

The four zones or phases begin with basic attitude and work assignments such as abiding by home and community rules, doing homework and refusing to given in to harmful impulses.

As attitudes improve, residents progress to a higher zone and accept more responsibility. They may become a big brother or sister to a resident in a lower zone, and each child has a counselor and a case worker.

During the past five months, 14 of the children have completed a reading tutoring

Article continues on next page…

program. Eight gained two years or better in ability, four were up an average of three months, one showed no change and one dropped two months.

Children at the home range from disturbed to borderline psychotic and from low to high mentality. None are severely anti-social, according to Jones.

"They are angry with themselves and their parents and have experienced failure in their homes. Some have multiple failures in foster homes," Jones said. "Much of the time kids work out problems in ways which harm themselves such as getting heavily into drugs.

"They all have poor self-concepts initially and we try to show them there are things they can do. We stress success instead of failure and encourage them to think about what they want to do with their lives."

Staff and residents work closely with schools and Jones emphasizes counseling doing much of it himself.

"We have no criteria and no screening committee," Jones explained. "We work for the need of the child."

At the same time, the children are putting forth an effort. For many, it is the first time.

Gain Privileges

Home visits are privileges, but it also is another effort toward growth. At home there are specific problems to be worked out and children report their progress when they return to the center. Previously, a home visit could mean a chance to be truant from school. It was a privilege to be abused.

Serious infractions of the rules in the center or on home visits result in drop in zone and loss of privileges.

In rap sessions, both the boys and the girls said they appreciated the trust they could earn and the activities.

They are pleased with the remodeling and happy with the discipline.

"It's helped me with my manners and behavior and I've stopped cussing," one boy said. That boy had been truant often from school, but has been going regularly and has found he likes it.

Until recently, Philip Allen was a case worker for Muskingum County Children's Services assigned to Avondale.

"Things have improved immensely," he commented. "The director is doing a good job. He understands children and methods and is doing a better job of handling the physical plant. The main thing is his understanding."

"The kids are more willing to talk about themselves and say what they feel," Allen said.

Work Together

Betty Gebhart, another social worker with Children's Services, found Avondale "more treatment oriented with the staff working together."

Avondale Treatment Center serves teenagers ages 13 to 18 with five professional staff and eight volunteer houseparents. It's annual budget is $125,569.

The average cost in the state per resident in a private non-profit treatment center is $50 a day. Avondale operates at $18 a day.

A break down of expenses is $72,469 a year for salaries; $29,000 for supplies such as food and clothing; $3,000 for equipment such as vacuum cleaners, furniture, refrigerators, etc.; $3,000 for travel allowances, spot labor and staff training.

"That's just the budget," Jones explained. "That doesn't necessarily mean we are going to spend that amount."

With Jones as director, the center is served by Joe Andrews, assistant director, who holds an assistant's degree in mental health technology.

Cynthia Rogers is activities-volunteer coordinator and will earn her mental health technology degree this year. Mildred Way, who has a degree in business, is a director and counselor and Claudia Wilson holds a bachelor of social work and is a child care supervisor.

Reap Benefit

Through hard work by the staff, but especially through efforts by the young people, things are looking brighter at Avondale Treatment Center. Improvements are reflected in the attitudes and achievements of the children and, after all, they are the ones to benefit most.

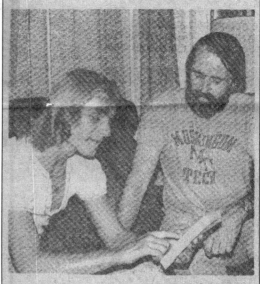

Ted Besser, left, works on reading skills in a tutoring session with Skip Myers, a houseparent at Avondale Treatment Center. The reading sessions and tutoring have helped improve student grades and increase student interest in attending classes. (Photo by Brian Dutro)

Charles Jones, director at Avondale Treatment Center, congratulates Gary Nichols on a trophy he won at Maysville Junior High School. Gary won the trophy for being the most improved person at the school during the past academic year. (Photo by Brian Dutro)

Above, Left & Opposite Page
Newspaper clipping, the *Times Recorder*, June 11, 1978.

Jill Brumage Bailey

I started working at Avondale Youth Center right out of college. I was 21 years old. Mr. Charles Jones was the Director and Claudia Wilson Hammack was my supervisor. Thank goodness while I was in college I worked part-time at a group home for delinquent girls or I would have fled that first week. I mainly worked the girl's side and they sure gave me a run for my money. Thank goodness for Claudia and Mr. Jones' guidance and advice. Mrs. Way was also one of my best gifts for guidance.

So many funny things happened on shift. I mainly worked with Tom Brown who worked the boys' side. For some reason the girls would come to me and confide all of their abuse issues, which meant that they trusted me. I seemed to have a good relationship with all of the girls. I learned that I couldn't be their friend, but I was there for them and they could count on me. They made me laugh and made me cry. We worked through the unimaginable hell that many of them had endured in their homes. Many of the girls had been sexually abused by different family members. One of the biggest questions I got was, "Why am I being punished and my family isn't?" My pat answer became that, " we need to keep you safe, and you are who is important to us".

I became the first Youth Leader III in Avondale's history. I did a lot of training when new staff came in to work at the center. I talked to 'newbies' about routine and structure. When a problem came up I confronted and dealt with it on the spot, but when I caught the kids making good choices I praised and gave lots of hugs.

When the girls came home from school I was there to greet them with hugs, jokes, ect. We would talk about their day at school good or bad. I encouraged the girls to help each other and praise each other which most of them did. The staff and kids cooked on the weekends, because it was the cook's day off. So the girls and I would go into the kitchen music blaring, singing and dancing while cooking. Then after dinner we would clean up the same way! That was a lot of fun! No matter what problems we had on our shift, I never let a child go to bed mad. I always tucked the girls in at night. They were so cute about it. Zone 1 & 2 went to bed at the same time so there were lots of sitting on the side of their bed telling them how awesome they were, and pulling the covers up to their chin after I gave them a hug. Kissing their

"I thought how neat it was that we had a pop machine in the kitchen. I could not imagine that from where I came from. Pop was only 15 cents for a bottle. I really liked going on trips, especially to the city, and picnics when all of the boys and girls could get together and have fun!"

Margaret Angler – 1977-78

forehead and saying goodnight, I love you and have a good day tomorrow as I switched off the light in each room. The greatest part of my job was watching a bunch of angry girls, who made poor choices, turn themselves around with a lot of encouragement. The encouragement came from everyone; Janet the secretary, Claudia, Mr. Jones, maintenance staff and the cooks. Patty Baker was the most fun and loving cook in the world.

The kids called me Jill-Z and to this day when they see me they come up saying hey Jill-Z and give me a hug. They tell me how they are doing and most of the time they are doing pretty good. I can honestly say that I saw the good in those girls and pointed it out to them.

I decided to leave not because I didn't like my job, but because I worked 11 ½ years of afternoon shifts full-time. I wanted day shift so I worked the rest of my career at Licking County Children Services. I missed being with those kids every day. I think Avondale helped lots of young folks become more responsible as adults who are raising healthy children. It gave them stability; they learned how to trust adults and how to have fun. Most of all they felt safe 24/7 while with us. Thanks for the memories.

– by Jill Bailey, Avondale Staff 1979-1990
Retired after 32 years of work in social services
(and still semi-sane).

Avondale Memories
by Rhonda Yoho
Avondale Resident, March 1982 – August 1982

One of my favorite memories is of child care worker, Tom Brown and I. Tom helped me create a Folgers Coffee commercial for a school project. It was the first time someone spent so much time with me for nothing more than homework, and I got an 'A' on the assignment!!!

I was also the first kid to make it to a Level 6 in the program. This was unheard of and I got to help make the rules for this level. I am very proud that I have a GED, own my own home and have raised a daughter who is now in college.

– by Rhonda Yoho

Big Sister Activities Organized

Friends of Children's Services has organized a "Big Sisters" program for the girls who live at the Avondale Children's Home, it was announced by Mrs. Melvin Krohn, chairman of the group. Big Sisters will also be selected for boys in the home who are under 12 years old.

Purpose of the program is to give each girl a special adult friend. Big Sisters will plan a meeting with their little sisters or brothers at least once a month, Mrs. Krohn said. In many instances, these meetings will mean the involvement of these youngsters in activities in the Big Sisters' homes. The adults will also help the youngsters in planning, selecting and repairing their clothing.

A get - acquainted meeting will be held at 1:30 p.m. Aug. 20 at the Children's Home. A highlight of the program will be a back - to - school fashion show in which the girls will model clothing they have made during the summer.

Friends of Children's Services is also continuing its collection of used clothing. Garments are stored in Central Presbyterian Church and distributed to children in the Children's Home and in foster homes in the county. Mrs. David Murray is clothing chairman.

Mrs. Dale Boyse is chairman of the Friends of Children's Home committee, assisted by Mrs. William VanGeison and Mrs. Krohn.

Above
Newspaper clipping, date unknown.

Above
Tom "Bubba" Brown, known for his unique humor and ability to connect with kids through his caring, compassionate nature and creativity.

Avondale Memories
by Bubba

A deeply personal and honest recollection and musings from a former houseparent of The Avondale Youth Center.

I came to the Avondale Youth Center in September of 1978.

I remember exactly what I was wearing at the time; green and yellow plaid flare-bottom pants and blue and yellow sneakers. It must have been difficult for my supervisor Claudia to keep a straight face when she saw me for the first time.

I'm sure in the back of her head she was thinking that I was exactly what would have happened if Goober Pyle and Janis Joplin had conceived a love child.

I didn't really know what I was getting into when I accepted the position as a live-in full time houseparent from then director Charlie Jones, who in turn didn't know what 'he' was getting into when he hired me in the first place. *For the record, other than camp counseling experience and one abysmal year as a teacher's aide, I had no experience whatsoever working with challenging kids in a residential treatment center.*

If I remember correctly, Charlie hired me because of my creativity. I had outlined my hand-written resume in bright colors and 3-D lettering. That impressed him, and somehow that led him to the conclusion that I would be an asset to the facility.

Mr. Jones saw something in me back then that I never knew was there in the first place. He must have felt that somewhere inside this rotund body covered with a 70's fashion nightmare, was the kind of heart and mind that could successfully work with tough kids.

After taking one look at me, I'm sure Claudia was looking at Charlie Jones, thinking that somewhere inside 'his' rotund head was a brain that was no longer functioning.

But of course, over time, she would see that I could handle this work with the best of them.

But it was never easy.

The challenges that came daily were immense. As a housepar-

ent, I felt that my job consisted basically of putting out little fires, one by one.

I'm sure the average parent puts out the same kind of fires; the difference here being that it involved twelve school-age boys, each with his own unique and amazingly complex personality.

And at first those boys knew how to work me, especially the older boys! On my first weekend as a houseparent, two of the craftiest teens came out into their living room to say that they were hungry.

I didn't think twice about it for a second. Minutes later we were all out in the kitchen and they watched with wide eyes (and grinning faces) as I prepared two 'huge' hamburgers loaded with cheese.

I'm sure all they wanted, or expected to get, was a candy bar or a little bag of chips. Instead, they got a T.B. Super-Burger; the size of which could completely clog the veins of an Alaskan Moose.

I can still remember those two guys, sitting there at that counter in junk-food nirvana, happily eating these giant burgers, a mountain of chips and drinking glass after glass of cold milk.

I can also remember the face of the girl's side houseparent as she entered the dining room and saw this 'feast' being consumed. She shot the two grinning boys a lethal look, and then quietly took

Above
Newspaper ad, c. 1979.

Notes
March 18, 1981: The Colony Square Mall opened featuring Sears, JCPenney and 40 other stores.

me aside and told me that I had been conned, and that all of this was against the rules.

I graciously thanked her for her guidance and wisdom, waited for her to leave and then opened up a box of Ho-Ho's so the boys had something to wash all that milk down with.

Now here's the thing: I didn't do this to be cool or for them to like me. I did this, because they said they were hungry and the one thing I could whip up fast was a hamburger.

I was fully prepared to be called on the carpet the following Monday. The girl's houseparent had cleverly put all the details of the illegal middle-of-the-night burger-bash into her logbook. Of course this info had absolutely nothing to do with her particular shift, but she wanted to make sure that the administration knew what I had done.

Nice try Nancy Drew. In the end, it didn't matter. Mr. Jones and Claudia thought that the whole thing was hilarious.

The cook at the time wasn't quite as jovial. Not being "Susie-Homemaker" in the kitchen, I had left the grill looking like I had tried to cook a side-of-beef, instead of just two hamburgers. Our cook at the time of my hiring was a woman of principle and she ran a tight ship in that kitchen. (I could have easily imagined her in another life as the burly cook on a battleship)

Holding onto her apron, quivering slightly, and using great restraint in her voice, she quietly but matter-of-factly showed me how to clean the grill properly.

She didn't care that I had cooked hamburgers for two boys in the middle of the night. I don't think she would have cared if I had cooked for the entire Mormon Tabernacle Choir that previous night. The fact of the matter was that I had made a mess in her kitchen and it was up to me to clean it up.

When I was done she was quite pleased, and I think she would have happily rewarded me with a fresh Ho-Ho … had there been any left.

At the time I think Claudia and Mr. Jones realized that I simply did what I thought was right at the time. Perhaps I had gone a tad overboard with the size of the 'snack', but my heart was in the right place nevertheless.

There was a lot of *heart* at Avondale. No one in his or her right mind did this work because of the money. Most of us were getting minimum wage.

The people that cleaned animal-poop at the shelter were getting more than we were.

Today, when I hear a teacher complain about how tough their job is for the money they are being paid, I have to smile. I want to say to that person: "You think *your job* is tough for what you're being paid?"

Try being a houseparent or a caseworker sometime. Try getting up in the middle of the night to go investigate the terrible abuse of a child or while you're at it, think about how hard it would be to hold back emotion when you see a new kid come to your place of work with everything he owns in the entire world ... packed in a garbage bag.

Try being a social worker or a house-parent for a few days.

Trust me, you'll happily RUN back to your job as a teacher like a Piranha to a meat-ball, and that crappy salary you go on and on about will suddenly feel like winning the lottery.

Nope, me and hundreds of thousands like me, never became houseparent's for the money. It might have started off as just a job that sounded interesting or a place related to a particular field of study, but if you stayed more than three months, it's because you now knew what you had gotten yourself into and you weren't going anywhere anytime soon.

You remained a houseparent on the staff at Avondale because that's what you wanted to do. You knew that it was not always going to be easy and you were prepared for just about anything during the course of a shift.

Sometimes you would fall into bed following a shift, mentally, physically and emotionally exhausted ... and hours later you got right back up to do it all over again.

None of us were there because we had any grandiose thoughts about changing the world either. And if anyone did think that, they were the ones that usually didn't last anyway, as did those that thought by letting kids break the rules, they would like you.

I experienced more than one newly hired houseparent work one shift and never return, simply because they couldn't handle it.

At Avondale you find out real fast just what it is like to work

---

Children Learn What They Live!

If a child lives with criticism,
He learns to condemn.

If a child lives with hostility,
He learns to fight.

If a child lives with ridicule,
He learns to be shy.

If a child lives with shame,
He learns to act guilty.

If a child lives with tolerance,
He learns to be patient.

If a child lives with encouragement,
He learns to be confident.

If a child lives with praise,
He learns to appreciate.

If a child lives with fairness,
He learns to seek justice.

If a child lives with security,
He learns to have faith.

If a child lives with approval,
He learns to like himself.

If a child lives with acceptance
and friendship,
He learns to find love in the world.

~ Dorothy Law Nolte ~

Above
Newspaper ads, c. 1979.

with sometimes-difficult kids in residential care.

You learn, sometimes within minutes, that these are not little orphans in diapers and sun-suits and the day is probably not going to end with all the kids joining hands and singing Kumbaya around a campfire.

However it was possible that if you listened carefully after bedtime, you could hear the strains of "Funky Cold Medina" coming from an aspiring young hip-hop artist in one of the rooms.

I never interfered with talking or singing after lights out. To this day I believe that bedtime should be a happy and peaceful time and if kids want to talk and sing a little bit to help them or others go to sleep, then so be it, especially if It helps them wake up feeling just as happy.

As a matter of fact, sometimes I would go from room to room after lights out and tell a joke or a short story of my own. There was no clause in the houseparent handbook saying I couldn't and I think the boys would have thought there was something wrong had I not done it.

It was part of my personality. I loved doing it. It was the one part of being a camp counselor that I was able to bring to Avondale.

Of course… It wasn't a full moon towering above the trees and a crackling campfire on a warm July night. Instead, it was a big messy room that smelled like an old grilled cheese sandwich with me in the middle of the floor telling stories and dumb jokes to a captivated audience of teenagers.

I can still hear those guys laughing.

While I'm sure that some facilities would frown on this, (and many other aspects of my personality) I was lucky enough to work at a place like Avondale. Luckier still was the fact that Mr. Jones and Claudia just about always went along with everything I came up with, as long as it somehow benefitted our kids and their stay at Avondale.

That's what really mattered.

What a lot of people don't know is that kids like those I worked with at Avondale, are really no different than other kids. In fact in some ways, they are better than so-called 'normal' kids. They appreciate things more, and they don't take things and people for

The first contribution to the 69th Avondale Children's Home Fund has been made by the Student Council of Maysville High School. Accepting the $50 check from Bill King, second from right and principal of Maysville High is Alan J. Leslie, publisher and general manager of The Times Recorder. With them are Sally Lemmon, The Times Recorder's Avondale Fund treasurer and Charles Jones, far right, director of Avondale Children's Home. Jones said the donation from Maysville students is special because Avondale residents attend Maysville schools. (Photo by Marjorie Trost)

TR Launches 69th Avondale Children's Home Fund Drive

Today The Times Recorder is launching its 69th annual Avondale Children's Home Fund to provide a Merry Christmas for youngsters there and special gifts throughout the year.

There are usually 18 adolescents at the home, which has a capacity of 24, according to Charles Jones, director. Avondale residents range in age from 13 to 17.

"Were it not for The Times Recorder Christmas Fund, the Avondale youth would be deprived of many of the special gifts, activities and opportunities available to other children," said Jones.

Money from the fund which is not used at Christmas is set aside for such activities as haircuts, school field trips, class pictures, birthday gifts, special clothing and movies. Other uses include roller skating, bowling, crafts and educational materials.

Jones said funds for such activities are not always available in Avondale's general operating funds.

Were it not for The Times Recorder's fund drive each year, there would be less of a Christmas and fewer activities and gifts for the children throughout the year.

Contributions may be sent to the Avondale Fund in care of The Times Recorder, Zanesville, Ohio 43701.

All donations will be acknowledged in a daily column.

Left
Newspaper article in the *Times Recorder*, November 11, 1980.

granted. Their life has often been tough. They have learned to fend for themselves and overcome adversity.

In an airport you can tell who the adults are that had everything given to them unconditionally while growing up, and the ones that were once in a residential facility like Avondale or had

Employees Honored

Awards were presented recently to Avondale Youth Center employees who have completed one or more years of service. Shown above are employees who have completed more than 10 years of service with the center. Left to right they are: Kay Extine, 15 years; Claudia Wilson, 12 years; and Charlie Jones, 11 years. Those with 1 to 10 years of service are pictured below. They include, left to right, Susan Alley, Patty Baker, Tom Brown, Janet Harper and Jill Bailey. Employees with 1 to 10 years of service who were not available for the photo are Cindy Shepard and Madeline Beckert. (TR Photos by Chris Kasson)

some tough breaks while growing up. Travelers with the tougher and more challenging childhoods are not the ones throwing a tantrum, followed by sucking their thumb, when the loudspeaker announces a forty-five minute flight delay.

So, over the years with incredible support from Mr. Jones and Claudia, I happily started and ran an in-house 5 – 8 Am radio station, held all-night volleyball parties over in the school-house, created a Halloween basement tour, conducted numerous movie marathons, supervised an in-house student newspaper, held nightly bedtime wind-down group sessions, and shortly after lights-out went into each room for about ten minutes and told a joke or a short story.

I also enjoyed shoving celery sticks up my nose to see if I could crack up Claudia during a stuffy board dinner in which no one was allowed to laugh, fell off a ladder into the bushes while trying to scare the kids by jumping up into the window with a face covered with flour during a Halloween movie, and stood on the boys roof late at night, and holding a fishing pole, lowered a candy-bar attached to a fish hook, against the window of a depressed kid.

It just seemed like the right thing to do at the time, and it made him smile and then laugh, which is exactly what I hoped would happen.

This is the first time I have ever told that story.

Frankly, it would take reams of paper to tell all the stories of what I did and remember from my eleven or so years at Avondale; seven of which I lived right upstairs in two rooms. One of those rooms was the radio station, and my mailbox downstairs was where the kids could put their requests and dedications ... *and every day they stuffed my mailbox with things they wanted me to say and play.*

As much as the kids (and <u>most</u> of the houseparent's) enjoyed the radio program, I enjoyed it even more. It wasn't always easy to drag myself out of bed at 4:30 to get everything ready by 5, but I did it almost every school day for three years ... *and I loved it.*

I loved so much about my job at Avondale.

It saddens me now to think that I eventually lost a lot of the spark that I had at the beginning. I reached a burnout point in year eight and found myself enjoying my work less and less. It wasn't

Above
Newspaper ad, c. 1979.

Opposite Page
Newspaper article in the *Times Recorder*, October 15, 1988.

Notes
May 6, 1983: The 4th Y-Bridge was razed by explosions as onlookers watched from Putnam Hill Park.

Above
Newspaper ads, c. 1979.

the kids. They were the best part of my job … most of the time anyway.

It was just that I was tired and ready for something different, and so since that time, I have made 26 educational films, been on over a dozen talk-shows and traveled all over the country and Canada talking to kids, parents and teachers about the problem of school bullying.

And if I could get in a time-machine and turn the clock back, I'd give it all up in a heartbeat … for a chance to be back at Avondale and start all over again.

I have learned that as we get older we always want to 'go back' to something that had value in our lives. We can't do that of course, so we have to rely on our memories to take us back.

The fact is, I'm often back at Avondale.

There has not been one day since; that for just a moment I haven't thought about the place and the people I worked with.

I think about the smile on the face of a boy or girl who were once filled with an almost incomprehensible degree of rage and fear… of the incredible feeling you get as a houseparent, while during a simple 1-to-1 with a stubborn and cynical kid, you realize you've just broken through the barrier between mistrust and trust.

I think of the umpteen big hugs I got from kids on zoning day, after I told them that they just went to the next level in the program.

I think about the sorrow on the face of a child, because I just happened to be right there when some bad news came from home.

I think about Jill-Z screaming at the top of her lungs as a huge bat was swooping down on her in the hallway by my bedroom upstairs.

I'm sure she was also quite annoyed when I chose to play '20 questions' about the species of the Bat, instead of immediately letting her in, which since I was already in bed, and didn't particularly want the 'Bat from hell' following her in, I chose to let her stay outside the door and scream.

I think about how quiet Avondale Youth Center was on Christmas Eve and Christmas Day. For all the years I was there alone during those hours, and only during those hours, the emergency line simply kept quiet... *as if no harm was allowed to come to a*

Charlie Jones, director of Avondale Youth Center, awards bonus points to two youths for their improved behavior. The amount of points a resident receives determines what category or "zone" the person is in and what their privileges may be. (TR Photo by Larry Rich)

child during this time.

I think about the "Welcome Home Bubba" sign that greeted me when I returned from a weekend stay in the hospital … and the cards and the balloons that were waiting for me in the office.

I think about how angry Mr. Jones was when he got a $10,000.00 bill from a Satellite company that I had placed an order with.

Charlie neglected to notice the date on the calendar.

I think about being trapped in an upstairs bathroom for two and a half hours, sitting on the toilet in my fruit-of-the-looms, on a cold morning, because for some reason the cleaning ladies

Above
Newspaper article in the *Times Recorder*, date unknown.

127

Above
Newspaper article in the *Times Recorder*, date unknown. Caption reads: "A member of Jones' staff counsels a child as the two walk into Avondale. Jones said his expert staff is what makes the children's home such a success."

Right
Newspaper article in the *Times Recorder*, November 8, 1989.

Ready To Run

Janet Harper, foreground, and Cynthia Hollingshead prepare for the fifth annual Avondale Youth Center Christmas Fund Run to be held at 10 a.m. Saturday, Nov. 25 in Avondale. There will be a five kilometer individual and corporate division race and a one mile fun run. Re- gistration begins at 9 a.m. and the fee is $5 pre-paid or $7 race day. Awards, t-shirts and ribbons will be presented. Proceeds will go to *The Times Recorder* Avondale Youth Center Christmas Fund. (TR Photo by Larry Rich)

decided to change their usual routine from doing the downstairs cleaning *first*.

I think about the good feeling I got whenever Mr. Jones commended me for something I did during a particular shift.

The fact is, all of us houseparent's loved getting his approval. We were like squirming hungry little puppies, and he was a giant teat.

In all seriousness, it was just that we gave so much of ourselves to the kids we worked with, without any or much thought of the good we were doing in the process, that a reminder from Mr. Jones or Claudia that they appreciated the work we were doing … *meant a lot*.

I think about how hard it was to pull a seventeen year old off a scrawny twelve year old, when during a TV documentary about an African village, the younger boy pointed to a large bare-breasted woman with rings in her nose and loudly declared that it was the older boy's mom.

I think about the time that the whole center witnessed a huge Red Triangle like thing float silently above us….and the next morning a rather put-off Mr. Jones coming into the building with his face red as a cherry, yelling like a madman while waving a newspaper in the air…a newspaper containing the article with a headline proclaiming <u>Avondale Youth Center Residents Report UFO</u>.

As I had been the one that called the report in to the F.A.A., I quickly disappeared into the safety of the kitchen and into Patty's pantry where I busied myself studying expiration dates on cans of lima beans.

I remember a little 12 year old with tears running down his face screaming "It's just a pair of scissors!" as I asked him to leave the volleyball game for drawing what I thought was something extremely inappropriate in the sand.

He had separated the closed blades a little too far from the round handles. Draw what I just described and I think you'll get the picture.

I remember the lump in my throat I always felt when kids said goodbye on their last day.

A lot of kids cried on their last day at the center, and hugged

Notes
November 9th, 1984: The 5th Y-Bridge opened.

Above
Movie reviews by Tom "Bubba" Brown in the *Zanesville Times Recorder*, c. 1982.

their peers and the staff before they left.

Some people in the community wouldn't understand that. They thought that Avondale was supposed to be some kind of junior-jail or a long-term detention facility that the kids weren't supposed to like.

Yes, we had our rules and there were consequences when a kid crossed the line or screwed up… but we were not a jail.

We were a home.

But probably the memory I'll always hold the closest to my heart was a phone call I received many years after leaving Avondale.

It came from a guy named Billy who had come to Avondale at the age of 12, blind in one eye, and feeling a lot of anger and sadness because he had been separated from his siblings. We bonded pretty fast and he trusted me implicitly. However, after learning some distressing news about his family one evening, he decided it was time to run away. I overheard him talking about it, and as bedtime drew near, I sensed that it was about to happen.

And I tried to stop it.

As he suddenly bolted from his bedroom, I confronted him about the mistake he was about to make. With tears streaming down his face, he begged me to leave him alone. In fact he told me that if I tried to stop him, he would hit me. He emphasized that he didn't want to hit me, but if I tried to stop him, he would.

And he did.

In fact the force of his little fist knocked my glasses right off my face. And then, realizing what he had just done, he crumpled to the floor and cried like there was no tomorrow.

The punch didn't hurt me.

What hurt was seeing this kid sobbing because he had just plowed into the one person who had always been there for him. Of course we were all there for him, but I was his buddy.

It took awhile, but I finally convinced him that I didn't take any of this personally, and the hit was relatively painless. Only when I assured him that I was still his friend, did he finally calm down.

But there was now a problem. How was I going to handle this

Above
A very homey, festive-looking dining room at the Avondale Children's Home. The less institutional-looking, the better it is for the home.

incident?

I didn't want to write him up, because hitting a houseparent was a serious offence and I knew that it would set him far back in the program. Next day I explained the whole situation to Mr. Jones and together we worked out a consequence that seemed fair, and while it illustrated that he had done wrong, it didn't bury him to the point of no return.

Claudia and Mr. Jones were great about working with house-parents who wanted the policies bent just enough, that in the end the consequences wouldn't hurt the progress we had made with a particular kid.

In the end it wouldn't have mattered, because just two days later we learned that a family in the northwest had accepted Billy and all of his brothers and sisters for adoption, and he was leaving for the airport early in the morning.

I was chosen to tell him the news, which was a tough thing for both of us. Fighting my own emotion, frustration and confusion due to the abrupt nature of all of this, I finally succeeded in con-

Above
Movie reviews by Tom "Bubba" Brown in the *Zanesville Times Recorder*, c. 1985.

vincing him that this was actually great news.

And it really was.

Being with his siblings was all that Billy had ever wanted in the first place.

We said our goodbyes and that was it. He was gone by the time I got up the next morning and I had learned a lesson about why you don't want to get attached to kids that you work with in residential care. It happens to many houseparents and it happened to me twice, and after Billy left, it didn't happen again.

But many years later he would call me from Florida; happily married and with kids that I could hear in the background. He had simply called to say hi and thanks for the good advice I had given him during his few months at Avondale.

I honestly don't remember what advice that was. It's easy to forget all of that as a houseparent, because we did it so much. Regardless if we remember the counsel we gave to the AYC kids or not, we didn't do it because it was part of our job. We did it, because it was in our heart to do it, and we didn't expect anything for it.

But more than two decades later, Billy decided to remind me that he had not forgotten.

And I'm pretty sure that many of the great houseparent's I have worked with, and thousands upon thousands just like them, have over the years been reminded of their value in the life of a child as well.

In closing …

To the current houseparent's at Avondale… I envy you.

To all those houseparent's and assorted AYC staff I worked with over the year's… thanks for the friendship and memories.

I especially want to thank those whom I worked with in the early days especially Mr. Jones and Claudia, for believing in me and my nutty ideas and putting up with a few lapses of good judgment …

Well, to be honest it was actually quite a few lapses of good judgment.

To my great friend Jill-Z. What times we had, huh?

And to my other fellow staffers and buddies: Janet, John, Eleanor, Kay, Barb, Cindy, Karen, Beth, Mr. Graham, Patty, Mary, Kevin, Jay, Denise …

(Really Denise, making my BVD's a part of a scavenger hunt was bad enough, but letting all those flies in my room? How do you sleep at night?)

… Herb who actually had a weirder sense of humor than me.

… and of course those people who are no longer with us; namely Skip and one of the greatest ladies I have ever known in my entire life: Mildred Way.

All of you were there when or soon after the adventure began and I will never forget you.

I also want to thank my old friends Hans Anderson, Bill Seyerle, Gary King who inspired me to write all this in the first place and Nate Norris, the guy I trained as a houseparent …. and look where he is now!

As for the kids I worked with during all those years, there are too many of you to single out. I just want to say that I hope I made a difference in your life … *because you sure made a difference in mine.*

I know that sometimes I was strict, seemingly unreasonable and I probably took the all-night volleyball tournaments a little too seriously, and probably played way too much hippy-dippy 60's and 70's music in the mornings … but I was only sharing with you, what made me happy in the first place; hoping it would make you happy as well.

Someday, years from now, maybe we'll all get together again in that great *youth center* in the sky.

We'll swap fond memories and have some laughs, and just like I used to do, I'll tell a few jokes and stories. It will be good times for sure.

And before we call it a day… *I'll make some big fat juicy cheeseburgers.*

– by Bubba, July 27, 2011

Above
Lind Arena public skating schedule, c. 1989.

Notes
1986: Lash High School was razed to make way for new development, including The John McIntire Library expansion and a new county building which would later house Children Services, The Muskingum Valley Educational Service Center, The Zanesville-Muskingum County Health Department and The Board of Elections.

Above
Mrs. Caughey and the two cooks.

The Cowboy, The Vitaphone and an 'Atomic' Mule

People have done their best from the earliest days to provide the Avondale kids with unique opportunities and gracious examples of generosity. In 1954, Film star Tim Holt made a personal appearance at the Children's Home. Tim Holt's film career took off after the 1939 classic Stagecoach followed by Orson Welles's The Magnificent Ambersons. Holt went on to become a decorated World War II combat veteran as a B-29 bombardier. The actor returned to cinema and starred in over 2 dozen more films including The Treasure of The Sierra Madre with Humphrey Bogart. During the 1940's Tim Holt ranked consistently as one of the top 10 favorite cowboy stars, and went as high as number 3. Over the next 20 years, the actor would only appear in several movies, with his final starring role in 'The Monster That Challenged the World'. During this time, Holt would make public appearance tours, attend rodeos and other events. On June 3rd, 1954 Holt was in town appearing at the Sky-Way Drive-In, on Maysville Pike, when he made a visit to Avondale. The visit included a pistol shooting demonstration on the Avondale back lawn.

In the 1940's the Avondale Home received the donation of a 'celebrity donkey'. Radio personality and Bob Hope sidekick Jerry Colonna sponsored a nationwide contest to 'name the donkey'. The winner of the contest was WHIZ radio announcer Ed Fisher who named the donkey, 'Atomic'. The donkey was flown from Los Angeles to Cincinnati then transported by truck to Zanesville. Atomic was made an honorary sergeant in charge of recreation by Marine Sgt. Ray Pennock during a special broadcast from the Muskingum County Fair, and then presented to Avondale Superintendent Jesse Hutson.

As early as the 1920's, donations and special events were documented in the newspaper. In 1926, a brief article mentioned that the 'kiddies' of the McIntire and Avondale Children's Homes were invited to the Muskingum County Fair, and that the fair board would ensure that they were entertained. The kids had a special treat in September of 1927 when they went to the Liberty Theatre to experience the Vitaphone. The Amrou Grotto arranged for the children to have an automobile ride to and from the theatre in which they would enjoy the newest technology for a 'Talkies' film. The vitaphone was one of the more successful attempts at syncing a record soundtrack to a film. An annual 'Orphan's Picnic' was held at Moxahala Park. However, it was canceled in 1929 due to the Scarlet Fever outbreak. Also, in 1929 The American Light Company, of downtown Zanesville, donated a 'huge radio'. It was listed a Zenith Model 8, one of the largest on the market at the time.

Christmas is a very special time for most children. Many kids spend the entire year looking forward to fun and joy that the holiday season brings. The sense of family, gifts and the anticipation of Santa Claus make Christmas a very exciting time for many children. However, Christmas at Avondale can be a difficult time. For a child that has little or no family, the holidays can be a time of great sadness and disappointment. Even the camaraderie they share with their peers is often lost, because some of the children will have visitors while others are only reminded of what they are missing. The 1924 Christmas Day edition of the *Times Recorder* reads "Christmas is really Children's day and will be celebrated as such at the Avondale home where at 7 O'clock this morning the children, numbering 75, will be admitted to the assembly room where a stately Christmas tree, laden with gifts, will gladden their hearts. These gifts were purchased through subscriptions received at the *Times Recorder* Office." Year after year for decades The *Zanesville Times Recorder* has held an Avondale Christmas fund. In December of 1937 a total of $152.79 was collected for the 59 children. In 1941 $246.52 was collected for the 80 children in the home. By the 1980's the collections have risen to the thousands annually. In the early days the fund was used primarily for Christmas gifts, but in the modern era it also pays for prom dresses, school sports fees and activities throughout the year.

Groups and organizations too numerous to mention have stepped forward to do everything from throw parties to build a picnic area on the grounds. The generosity of the public towards Avondale has been inspiring from the very beginning to present day.

Above
Staff member, Mary Thagard, during a light moment at the Children's Home.

Education

The educational pursuits of the children at the Avondale Children's Home were initially and for several decades served by an on-site, two room school house with a minimum of teaching personnel. Children were taught a no-frills, basic curriculum of fundamental reading, writing, and arithmetic courses. Developmentally and age appropriate teaching was, in fact, attempted but

"My great grandmother, Goldie Sharrer, was also a resident of Avondale during the 1950s. Avondale has made me the man I need to be to be successful!"

Ryan Robinson – 2005-11

Notes
Moxahala Park was an amusement park opened in 1927 complete with roller coaster, ferris wheel, ballroom and other attractions. It operated nearly half a mile from the Avondale Home until around the early 1980's.

The American Light Company celebrated its 100th Year Anniversary in 2010.

with few teachers and exceedingly large numbers of students to be taught, individualized education and educational specificity was not always possible.

The Avondale Youth Center adheres to the educational philosophy that children deserve, whenever possible, school attendance at their own neighborhood school. Some children while placed at Avondale do continue their education at the school that they attended at the time of their placement. Most, however, do attend the local school district which happens to be the Maysville Local District. Children are oftentimes offered the opportunity, if meeting the minimal requirements, of attending the communities Mid-East Ohio Vocational School. For children experiencing violent, self-destructive mental health issues and needing to be admitted to the Child Psychiatric Unit at Bethesda Hospital, there is our on-site education component administered by the Muskingum Valley Educational Services Center that attempts to create continuity and continuation of their home school education experiences. In exceptional cases, children may attend the Excel Academy in Newark, Ohio. Furthermore, Foxfire School has recently offered many Avondale children an excellent educational alternative. The vast majority of children currently and most recently placed at Avondale have an Individualized Educational Plan (IEP) that attempts to secure a personalized, efficient academic plan for each individual child.

Avondale Youth Center Offers Values, Standards To Children

By CHRISTOPHER BARTON
Staff Reporter

Ten years ago a child care counselor acted more like a "police officer" and did not have to be as dimensional when it came to dealing with juveniles.

Charlie Jones, director of the Avondale Youth Center, says nowadays a counselor must possess leadership qualities and remain optimistic, involved and committed to a teen's problems.

"The values, standards and ways of living are not available to them in their family setting," says Jones of the 20 kids at the center, some of whom were emotionally and sexually abused.

Jill Brumage, a 9-year veteran counselor, adds when she began working there, kids would abuse drugs, be truant and fill the "gang member" stereotype.

Today "it's more complicated when it comes to counseling and dealing with them," she explains.

Karen Jones-McKee, a second year counselor, says she realizes the goal of the center is "to reunite the childen with their families if at all possible.

"But I feel like for some of these children, the best thing for them is not to be reunited with their biological family," she adds.

Jones-McKee says, "We have had kids who have done excellent here" but when they return home they continue the patterns they learned at home.

"We see them a month or two later, and it's like we never had them," she says of the kids who go home and come back to visit. "They learn while they're here, but it's easy for them to get back on their parent's influence again."

Jones points out that Avondale is a home to children and "families feel comfortable because (the center) is not a competing family."

More work must be done with the families, he admits, informing them of their child's progress and "strengthening the families so they can take care of their kid."

Future projects include establishing an after-care program and coordinating an independent living program for teens ages 17-18.

Besides family, Jones said he believes the military is a positive place for the teens to turn after Avondale. Jim Arbuckle, a former resident at the center, is now in the Army.

At least two girls have plans to go into the armed forces. But some live alone or get married and have children.

"After they leave and come back and tell you how great things are or show you their kids, that to me is the biggest highlight," say Brumage.

Above
Newspaper article from the *Times Recorder*, date unknown.

Finding a Home

During the first half-century of the opening of the Avondale Children's Home, children would enter the home at various ages ranging from newborn to late teens. Without the advantages of the philosophy of child welfare, which is employed today, and without the contemporary tool bag of services, children placed at the Avondale Children's Home during the early years were typically left to "age out" or emancipate (using current language) at the home.

Current statistics at the Avondale Youth Center show an aggressive posture of finding safe, stable, and loving traditional homes for children as quickly as possible. Average length of stay at the Avondale Youth Center in early 2010 stands at 6 ½ months.

Children are consistently and successfully emancipated back to biological parents, professional foster homes, adoptive homes, kinship provider homes, and guardianship placements. The philosophy that every child deserves and demands a traditional nuclear home reigns true. As the government agency charged with the noble task of protecting children from abuse, neglect, and abandonment, the work of modern child welfare must be accomplished in a very timely manner and by always serving the best interests of the child in the least restrictive environment as possible.

Medical & Dental

Advances in medical and dental care exploded throughout the 20th century and into the 21st century. This statement of fact directly related to the children's experiences at Avondale during the past 100 years. The early years of medical and dental care at Avondale were rather basic (some may say primitive) and not at all proactive or preventive in nature. In terms of dental care, there was no fluoride in the natural spring water and dental hygiene was not at the top of the list of priorities (at least until one had a toothache); therefore, dental issues were abundant and the intervention techniques could be classified as crude. Medical care was administered on a "when the child is sick" basis and, at the time, immunizations to many dreadful diseases were not yet available. Influenza outbreaks, tuberculosis, strep throat, measles, etc. were all unfriendly, unwelcome guests at the Avondale Children's Home. The cemetery at the south side of the facility is a devastating, catastrophic testament to the same.

Medical and dental care improved throughout the decades with the advent of many outstanding initiatives. Fluoride in our water sources, proactive wellness strategies, vaccines, and immunizations all but eliminated many dreaded diseases, and laws and regulations were written into child welfare policy requiring appropriate, professional medical and dental intervention strategies.

Current practice at the Avondale Youth Center requires that each child upon entering the facility receive a medical screening by a physician or nurse practitioner within five (5) working days. Furthermore, all children must then receive a comprehensive, physical examination within sixty (60) working days of entering care.

"Children Services and Avondale has helped me a lot. I still need to work hard to make sure I can do good. This is a nice place."

Raymond Graham – 2007-11

Treatment

Professional treatment services in the early years were, in many ways, limited to providing a spiritual and structured environment coupled with work expectations for the children in residence. Three hots (meals) and a bunk (a bed) was the order of the day. Food, shelter, meeting daily living needs, and the development of an individual civil code of conduct was the treatment milieu. Discipline and behavior management in the early days was administered swiftly and what could be considered now as rather harshly. Paddling with a board or switch was rather commonplace. Creating excessive work experiences and/or lifestyle deprivation were a means by which order and individual personal development were attained.

Such personal descriptors as imbecile, incorrigible, unsanitary, bastard, and half-breed were used to describe residents in official documents. While the aforementioned words and descriptors were certainly a part of the larger lexicon of the time in the early 20th century, their use makes us shudder today.

We now use words such as unruly, traumatized, mania, socially-isolated, depressed, handi-capable, hyperactive, delinquent, abused, and many more to describe children and treatments.

A behavior modification model of points and levels used to reinforce positive behavior and extinguish negative behavior was introduced at the Home in the 1970s. The simple idea that if you do good things, good things will happen to you was the mantra and the ultimate hope for staff and children alike. Children on lower levels with less compliance had less freedom of choice and movement while, conversely, children who earned higher levels due to more compliance had much greater freedom of choice and movement.

Currently, children are sponsored by a staff member who serves as a mentor, coach, and advisor. Treatments for ADHD, mental health issues, and other diagnosed maladies requiring medication are strictly overseen and prescribed by a physician. Family-centered, strength-based treatment is the treatment modality of choice with individual, group, and family counseling provided. Family support groups have been organized and offered since 2000. Treatment that works is sought and administered as it is widely recognized that different children require a wide range of varying treatment strategies.

Notes
1993: Minor League Baseball returned to Zanesville with the 'Zanesville Greys'.

Charlie Jones leaving post as Avondale Center director

By CHRISTOPHER BARTON
Staff Reporter

AVONDALE — Avondale Youth Center is losing a vital member of its staff who has helped provide "magic" for troubled children since 1977.

Charles G. Jones, youth center director, started at the old children's home on Ohio 93 where children continually ran away. Since then, he has helped turn their lives around.

He is retiring early from this job, but is eager to begin working in a similar capacity with a group of Zanesville psychiatrists.

"I came very close to working here into my '60s," said Jones, very active at 53. "I think I'll be able to concentrate my skills, whatever I have, to do different and more challenging things."

This fall, Jones will join Ohio Psychiatric Associates at Doctor's Park, Bethesda Hospital. He leaves Avondale, Oct. 11.

Jones has 25 years of counseling experience, a degree in experimental pyschology and experience as a probation officer and past Zanesville Youth Camp counselor.

As Jones talks about the success he and a staff of 14 have brought to Avondale, he ultimately is torn at leaving behind adolescents who come here with "no chance" for a productive life.

Avondale has no delinquent high school students and all have been promoted and graduated. Many children find the longer they stay at Avondale, from nine months to one year, the more successful they become. The biggest problem is nudging teens into the real world after they have learned to deal with their problems shared by peers.

"We have had a lot of pressure to keep kids in here in the last five years. That's the primary reason for our reputation," Jones said. "It's gotten easier because we keep a fairly stable staff who are really talented."

The home is governed by Muskingum County Children's Services and is funded by tax levies. Jones said he's happy that the board of trustees has let him run the show.

Avondale's staff must cope with young thoughts of suicide and drugs and 15-year-olds who could be dangerous to themselves or others, although no teen has physically harmed anyone at the home, Jones said.

Jones utilizes a behavior modification program where 14- to 18-year-olds are treated with respect and given some sense of responsibility. Avondale presents a family-like atmosphere where staff works closely with the teens.

Above & Opposite Page
Newspaper article in the *Times Recorder*, September 10, 1991.

Right
Director, Charlie Jones honoring one of the many youth to graduate the Avondale Program, which he designed.

Charlie Jones clowns with Claudia Hammack, clinical services director at Avondale Youth Center. Jones is leaving to take a position with Ohio Pyschiatric Associates. (Times Recorder Photo by Christopher Barton)

"Kids can change," Jones said. "But each year it's more difficult to get through adolescence."

Dale Curry, tutor for Avondale youth at Maysville High School, said her classroom has been an easier place to work because of cooperation from house parents at Avondale.

"They build confidence and security through the program," said Curry, who after six years is noticing improvement in student's attitude. "I have never had a situation where I haven't had support."

Years ago people could easily identify Avondale students, she said, but it's a great compliment when someone does not realize that a student spent time at the home.

Jones even marvels at how well the kids do in school. When released from Avondale, they are placed in foster care, live independently or may enter the U.S. Armed Services.

Some children are placed through Muskingum County Juvenile Court, but they don't necessarily have a criminal record if they stay there. Many are depressed or have emotional problems.

Beth Prather, juvenile probation officer, is one person who will miss Jones and his influence on teens.

"He's so good with our kids. He has a knack of getting a child to open up and get to the heart of the problem," she said. "He re-

ally gives us a pretty good idea of what kids will work at the home. I think that's why he has success. He has created that position and it will be hard to fill."

Claudia Hammack, the clinical services director at Avondale, said "Charlie has been supportive and extremely talented in working with the kids." She hopes the center will carry on in his tradition.

Jones said he will miss hearing from those who have stayed at the center, started families and thankfully visit or call in.

"I will be thinking about the staff and kids," he said. "Many times they give back more than you can give them."

By RICK SCHLUEP
Staff Reporter

"I tried to kill myself and I was into drugs," the child spoke softly. "I couldn't communicate with my parents so I took drugs to escape. I was put into a hospital for my drug problem and I tried to kill myself."

The preceding is a profile of a person who was a resident of Avondale Children's Home on Roseville Road.

The character sketches that follow are of former residents of the home who have dramatically changed in both lifestyle and attitude since their entrance there.

As for the child mentioned above, being at Avondale resulted in her abstinence from drugs, her being able to have long-lasting relationships and she doesn't hate her parents any more, she said.

"I want to get into something to help people. Being there helped me decide on my career," she stated.

But leaving the home was another story, because she explained, at Avondale "a lot of people have to put up with your problems."

Communicating Stressed

At Avondale, "the whole program is based on constructive communication," said Charles Jones, the home's director.

Jones has a staff consisting of a secretary, maintenance man, cook and laundress, child care supervisor and full-time and part-time youth leaders.

The staff works with children who have various problems, such as the following girl who resided at the home. "What brought me here was me. I was running the streets all the time and I was real down on myself — enough to try and kill myself," she recalled.

Being at Avondale helped her learn that she needed to try and understand her parents. Plus, she said, her attitude changed dramatically to where she likes herself now.

Whether addicted to drugs or being a runaway, all the children get treated the same, one resident stated. "They (outsiders) make it sound like a prison, but it isn't. You get all treated the same here, except for the priveleges, which you have to earn," she added.

Earning Advancement

New residents of the home enter into Zone 1a. Progressing through a zone is done on a point system in which the child must earn 75 percent of the points to advance from 1a to 1b, then from b to c and so forth, Jones said.

A child needs 80 percent of the points to progress through Zone 2; 90 percent is needed in Zone 3; but no grading takes place in the fourth and final zone. Points are awarded when a child meets specific goals.

To jump from one zone to another, such as from 1c to 2a, each candidate for such a move must be evaluated by the other children. The written reports then go to the staff which decides whether that child should advance.

With an advance, the child receives more priveleges and moves into better living quarters. The entire operation is reality-oriented, Jones said, where goals are established for the children to meet. Usually, a child can progress through the zones and leave Avondale within four to six months, he added.

Before the children are accepted into Avondale though, they are interviewed by Jones. "I have to have the feeling we can help the kids."

And helping problem children is the meaning of Avondale and those talked to relate how they have been helped. "I've learned responsibility between people and I'm taking care of things better now," the youth stated.

Continued on 6-A

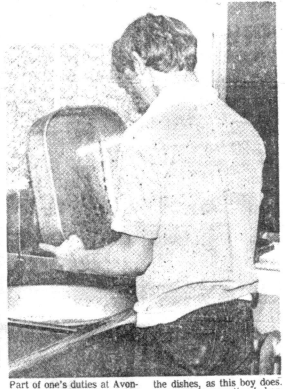

Part of one's duties at Avondale Children's Home is doing the dishes, as this boy does. The home's operation is based on constructive communication, while also being reality-oriented.

Playing with a computer word game in the living room of the home is one small part of the home's positive teaching philosophy.

Sometimes, part of the day's activities includes a game of volleyball. The home's director, Charlie Jones, attempts to score a point.

Jones counsels a girl in his office. The director said that his staff keeps things light and warm at Avondale, providing a positive atmosphere.

Opposite Page & Left
Newspaper article in the *Times Recorder*, date unknown.

Above
Patty Baker. More than just a cook, Patty's sense of humor and motherly nature impacted hundreds of kids and staff.

Patricia Baker

I am writing this for my beautiful friend and co-worker Patricia Baker. She was the cook at Avondale for 25 years. I actually stole her from another establishment to come to work with us. What a find. Patty became the heart of Avondale. It was the enticing smells that drew you in and her infectious humor that filled your soul. She always began each conversation with "let me tell you a story babe".

Patty pampered staff and youth alike. Patty could sense when someone needed to talk. She was quick with a smile or a hug and just as quick with the proverbial "kick in the rear-end". I can still walk into the kitchen and hear her say "I am going to teach you something your mother should have".

No one could forget the holiday meals she served. Patty was insistent about every child experiencing the excitement of a holiday dinner with all the trimmings and the closeness it brought. Even when she had a simple dinner of hamburgers and french fries (a teenager's favorite) we were treated to homemade apple pie and ice cream for dessert. Oh, let's not forget her special treat of *monkey bread,* a dessert us Avondale folks will long remember.

There are times when it is a challenge to keep your sanity while working with 22 teenagers and many a time Patty would take a child, who was close to exploding, into her kitchen. She had just the right recipe to calm them down. She was a child care workers best friend. You can't put into words why Patty was respected, she just was. Staff, parents and youth all learned from her and loved her dearly.

Patty retired in 2006. When kids come back to Avondale, to visit, they always want to see her. When we tell them she retired they are disappointed for themselves but more for the current kids that will not have the experience of such a special person.

– by Janet Harper, Indirect Services Coordinator 1979-Present

Claudia Hammack

I was fresh out of college when a friend told me about an opening at the Avondale Youth Center. I was hired as a house parent for the girls. I was naïve and clueless about working with adolescent girls. After all, I had majored in Social Work so I could change the world! I guess I was going to begin with this small group of street smart and troubled girls. Richard Evilsizer was the director at that time. Shortly, Charles Jones assumed directorship and he instituted a more therapeutic treatment program based on behavior modification techniques. That's when my real education began. He taught all of us how to effectively work with adolescents. He gathered a team of staff to turn angry, scared kids into being open to the possibility of a better future. We started with the basics. When a child would arrive at the center we would take them to K-Mart for new school clothes. Their medical/dental needs were attended to. That began the journey of feeling like maybe this wouldn't be such a bad place. Other kids befriended them, staff engaged them in positive encouragement and they received good, home cooked meals! For many, this was their first experience of feeling safe, successful and free from whatever chaos was occurring in their home.

I graduated to being the Staff Supervisor for the majority of my time at Avondale. It is by far the best job I have ever had. What fun we had! Yes, there were days when it was a challenge to maintain your sanity while kids were acting-out and making it their mission to give everyone a huge headache. But, most of the time it was fun and rewarding. One of the staff, Tom Brown, used his unique sense of humor to diffuse situations, put kids at ease and keep us all in stitches. I came to work on Sunday afternoon. Tom called me to the boys' living room and told me he and one of the boys had been able to film a strange occurrence the night before. They proceeded to show me a grainy video of a disc shaped object hovering over the back field that they filmed out of a window. I was not excited and had images of alien abductions! They kept me going for awhile till my suspicions made them reveal it was an old rubber bathtub stopper suspended from fishing line.

Other memories that stand out are the fashion shows we had. Each school year, the kids would put on their favorite new outfit. The boys, especially, enjoyed dressing like rock stars and lip-syncing to 'Guns & Roses' and popular songs of the day. We filmed them and they got a kick out of watching it back. I have to mention that I was the resident beautician for many years. I had three standard cuts so everyone walked around with the same hairdo. I was not trained, but look at all the heads I could practice on! I only made one girl cry when she looked in the mirror. When a youth was ready to leave, we would have a graduation ceremony. A special dinner was held, family was invited and speeches were

Notes
1994: 'The Wilds' opened the public.

Above
Janet and Kay hard at work on their administrative duties.

Notes
1996: Good Samaritan Medical Center and Bethesda Hospital began the process of merging into Genesis HealthCare System.

prepared. Mr. Jones always delivered the best graduation speech reflecting on the child that arrived and the changed one that was leaving that day. We always cried. I worked in the evenings when the kids were home from school. My role was often disciplinarian and I was charged with making sure the program was implemented as it should be. I felt like I had the best of both worlds, the ability to work with both staff and kids. We were blessed to have numerous talented, caring and committed people throughout the years. Many of us have remained friends throughout the years.

After Mr. Jones retired I was Interim Director for 9 months. I am proud of what I accomplished during that time of transition, but being more comfortable as 'second fiddle' I was glad to welcome Gerald Brandt to Avondale. Mr. Brandt brought new ideas to further our development as a diversified treatment center. I later made the difficult decision to move on after 19 years with the center. I chose Nate Norris as my replacement and it's no surprise he is now the Director.

I live in Florida and often wonder about the kids that passed through Avondale and how their lives have turned out. I have a lot of picture albums filled with class photos with inscriptions of appreciation on the back, group photos of kids with staff and events chronicling my experience at the center. Not all of those kids were able to avoid the pitfalls of mistakes and poor judgment. Or repeating the patterns of dysfunction learned from family. But, if they were able to remember a time when their needs were met, they felt safe, cared about and experienced a sense of pride then our mission was accomplished. If others were able to persevere, apply the lessons that they learned to their own lives and draw upon strengths to be successful, however they define that, then it is cause for celebration. It's difficult to convey the uniqueness of being part of the Avondale Youth Center experience. An experience the public doesn't really get to see and appreciate. Hopefully, one will get a better sense from reading the stories and tales compiled here. My story is in memory of Mildred Way and Dale Curry.

– by Claudia Hammack, Avondale Staff 1976-1996

Above
Bubba, Claudia and Mr. Jones.

Left
Newspaper article about Patty Baker's husband "Bake," who was a beloved volunteer for many years

Taking root

These teens at the Avondale Youth Center planted a tree, donated by Timber Run Garden, at the center last week as a memorial to long-time youth center voluntee Willis Baker. Sixteen students have been involved in the center's summer prog- ram, which has included visits to the Ohio District Council Nursing Home and preparation of a comforter for the Salvation Army. (Times Recorder Photo)

Gerald E. Brandt
Remembering a Return to the Future

When I started at the Avondale Youth Center, in April, 1992, accepting the position was somewhat of a 'return to the future' for me. I began my career in social work (after a brief stint teaching high school) at the Warrendale Youth Development Center, just north of Pittsburgh, PA. The facility, just acquired from the county by the state of PA, was a large institution for delinquent youth aged 10 through 23, from all parts of the state. I returned to this facility as a supervisor after acquiring my Masters at West VA Univ. And I believe that it was this experience and my success there that laid the foundations for the balance of my career in social work. There was a brief deviation into the restaurant business (definitely a learning experience!) but I quickly returned to the work I preferred.

In many ways, Avondale was reminiscent of my work at Warrendale. Youth were more amenable and they were younger at Avondale; but the issues were similar and sometimes, because of the complexity of the families from which they came, the problems seemed more challenging to resolve.

I vividly remember my first introduction to Avondale. I was asked by the Executive Director to meet with the staff---prior to receiving a final offer for the position. I was anxious! When I entered the building, no one seemed to be there. I literally wondered the halls for what seemed like an endless period of time. It was certainly an effective way of raising my anxiety even further.

My first observation was that the building seemed dark and depressing; I was having second thoughts! Finally the Executive Director found me and invited me to meet the staff---all of them together in one room. They had tons of questions none of which I had anticipated. So, after an hour and a half, I was thanked and waited in the hall. Shortly, the Exec. Dir. asked me to join him in his office at the downtown building. I truly was not optimistic nor was I certain that this was what I wanted (A major cultural change from Pittsburgh).

After quite a long conversation, I agreed to take the position and began on April 27, 1992 (a day that will live... NO, not really!).

My experience at Childrens Service/Avondale was the most rewarding and satisfying I have ever had. Both the people at

Notes
1997: Zanesville Celebrated its
200th birthday.

Director named at Avondale center

Gerald E. Brandt has been named director of the Avondale Youth Center.

As the former executive director of Opportunities and Resources of Pittsburgh, Pa., he brings proven management skills, counseling skills and staff training skills to the youth center. His background offers a unique combination of institutional and community experience with adolescents, their families, the courts, and with various therapeutic intervention techiques.

Brandt holds a bachelor of science degree from Xavier University and earned his master of social work degree from West Virginia University. He has been the executive director of Opportunities and Resources Inc. for 15 years. O.A.R. was incorporated in Allegheny County, Pa., under a board of directors composed of volunteers from the area's business and service communities. Opportunities and Resources was founded to enter contracts to recruit and counsel youths for CETA job training.

The city of Pittsburgh later contracted with O.A.R. to run a graduate equivalency (GED) program. Ninety percent of their clientele get jobs or enter advanced training. Each year the agency assesses and provides counseling to over a thousand applicants to the city of Pittsburgh's federally funded training programs. The agency also assisted persons in career development.

Brandt has been a free lance consultant since 1970. He has conducted training programs in management, organization, quality control, fund raising, systems analysis as well as other topics for business and service corporations. He was the training director for the Youth Development Center of Warrendale, Pa., and has been a part time college instructor for Indiana University of Pennsylvania for the past 20 years.

Brandt feels that he will make an excellent director of the Avondale Youth Center. He desires to make this career change so that he may have a more direct child and family counseling responsibilities, a smaller staff and continue in the field of administration. He feels his administrative and program development skills had moved him too far from the client and line staff at O.A.R. He believes that he is "coming home" to his counseling roots at the Avondale Youth Center.

GERALD E. BRANDT

Avondale and those at the main office were consistently supportive, open to suggestion, willing to challenge and constructively criticize, and simply fun to work with. The youth and families throughout the years were a constant and simultaneous source of frustration and joy. I believe that, together, we made significant impact in many lives. And I believe that that continues at present.

And, although I did love being at Avondale, I do indeed love being retired!!

– by Gerald E. Brandt, MSW, Director 1992-2008

Above
Newspaper article in the *Times Recorder*, May 16, 1992.

Gary King

After about my third week working at Avondale, I sat at home after a particularly rough 3-11 shift and thought to myself, "I have to stay for at least one full year". Any less than that would be giving up, my father had served two tours of the Viet Nam war so I should be able to handle one year of working with teenagers. Nearly nine years later I finished my last shift as an Avondale employee. I found myself standing alone in the dining room at the center, not quite sure how to leave for the last time.

The first year was very tough, as it generally is for most Child Care Workers. For those who work there very long, Avondale tends to become ingrained into your lifestyle and deeply affects you as a person. Just like many others in the past, it is where I met my wife and many of my closest friends. Through Avondale I was able to finish my formal education, but also received a more important education about the struggles many people go through and a different side of life to which I had never been exposed.

Since my start in the mid-nineties through the present day I have known many great staff. Unfortunately, the nineties and beyond are only briefly touched on in this book and too many things have happened to be done justice here. That history is still being written and can best be seen by visiting one of the many public events, finding a way to become involved with the kids at Avondale or just taking a moment to thank the staff for their remarkable work. The current staff are some of the hardest working people that I know. This is the only childhood that these youth have, and it is an absolute priority that they get the most out of it. I think that most who have worked at Avondale feel that their time there was the 'golden era', but that is just a testament to what a great place it has been for such a long time.

– by Gary King, Avondale Staff 1996-2005

Nathaniel Norris

Twenty three years ago I embarked upon a wonderful journey that has taught me many life lessons; Lessons in the strength of human character, the potency of prayer, and the courage and perseverance of young people who face many difficult challenges. This journey has taught me that family is more than a biological connection; it is deeply caring about the well being of others. Over the past twenty three years I have had mentors that have helped shape and guide my journey. Charlie Jones, the first Director that I worked for, had a special way of connecting with kids. They wanted his approval and no matter what discipline Charley handed down, the kids came out of his office knowing he was there to help and that he cared for them. I continue to admire that quality and to incorporate his unique style in my everyday approach.

Claudia Hammack, the Interim Director after Charlie, was an inspiration to me as well. I remember an occasion at dinner when one of the kids didn't finish eating the food on their plate. Claudia said; "We don't want to waste good food", and with that, she ate the food herself. What mother hasn't done that for their own child? I remember thinking, wow, she just showed the kids that

ATTN TO:
The Staff of Avondale Youth Center
& Children Services of Muskingum County

I wanted to thank you all for the wonderful care package you all put together. I especially enjoyed the notes from the kids. That put a huge smile on my face. It still does, everyday I open my wall-locker and see them hanging there. Knowing I have the loving and caring support from all of you, it makes being here and doing what it is I'm doing while here in Iraq, much more worth the while.

I truely love the country, to which I call home. The Great Land of Ladie Liberty - Our country that holds the brightest beacon of freedom. No matter hard times get or how bad things might seem to get, I will always Love our country. Always proud to call myself an AMERICAN. I will do anything it takes to protect her and the one's I love the most that reside in her. To me, THERE IS NO FLAG TO WHICH FLIES HIGHER AND WAVES MORE BEAUTIFULLY THAN OUR OWN AMERICAN FLAG!!!

So in closing, I thank you all for your loving and caring support. It truely means the world to me. I get a chance to come home sometime late January, early February, for 2 weeks. I will most definitely make an opportunity to come there and pay a visit. Until then, keep thanking every soldier you see for their service, Stay Safe, and keep the smile's on the childrens face's.

Sincerily:

SGT JASON ECKERTSON
AKA "THE SARGE" + "E-DOG"

Trevor Jones, Times Recorder

Nathaniel Norris stands in one of the meeting rooms of Avondale Youth Center. Norris has worked at the home for 21 years and has been director for the past three years.

NATE NORRIS

AGE 45

BIRTHPLACE Zanesville

EDUCATION Bachelor's degree from Ohio University in sociology and philosophy of religion; graduate degree from Ohio University in Lancaster in public administration.

OCCUPATION director of Avondale Youth Center

COMMUNITY INVOLVEMENT President of the Muskingum County Board of Health; president of Leila Payton Counseling Center; member of the Ohio Association of Child and Youth Care Professionals; member of executive board of Boy Scouts of America; advisory board member for the Social Work Program at Zane State College; and active in The Church of God and Saints of Christ in Zanesville.

Youth center director active throughout community but keeps focus on kids

BY KATHY THOMPSON
Staff Writer

ZANESVILLE — Nate Norris thinks if you fail at something, you keep on trying.

"You don't give up," said Norris, director of the Avondale Youth Center. "You keep on trying. I've believed since I was little that if you have a dream, you can do it."

Norris, who has been at Avondale for 21 years and director for the past three years, said he has devoted his life to giving back to his community and trying to help young people see the difference between right and wrong.

Although Norris does not have any children of his own, he has been instrumental in raising three nephews.

"We're a very big family here in Zanesville," Norris laughed. "There's a lot of us. We all love each other very much and help each other out. That's what families are for. It's one reason I appreciate living in Zanesville. It's small town enough that my family can stay close and be together often."

Norris stays busy with his activities not only at Avondale, but also on various boards and in support groups throughout the community. Norris is president of the Leila Peyton Counseling Center and runs a support group for that organization.

"We're trying to keep the kids on track," Norris said.

Norris is also president for the Muskingum County Health Department and would like to see a "healthier community."

"What I mean by healthier is that the drug problem has seemed to grow so much in the past few years," Norris said. "It's not only a huge problem here in Zanesville, but throughout the entire country. I would just like to see our kids stay away from the drugs and show them there's a better way, even if it's a harder way sometimes."

Norris said he thinks young people are more influenced by outside sources today.

"Kids just seem to be more damaged then before," Norris said. "They're making a living selling dope. You see a child when they're in middle school and the next time you see that child, they're in high school, but it's been a complete drop in their lifestyle. They've gotten into trouble and see no other way."

Norris developed his deep devotion to the community while watching his grandfather, Edger Norris, build the Church of God in Zanesville.

"Even though I was a little kid, that so impressed me," Norris said. "My grandfather was the minister, and the congregation had been trying to get a church built for years. Then my grandfather stepped in, and everyone pitched in and it got built. He believed in doing what you had to do, doing what you could do and doing what needed to be done."

Although Norris thought about becoming a minister, he decided he could make more of a difference in lives if he worked at Avondale.

Norris said he strongly thinks one person can make a huge difference in lives.

"I feel that working with abused and neglected children is sort of a ministry and every day

article continues on next page…

...article continued from previous page

NORRIS

brings about hope for the future," Norris said. "As Mahatma Gandhi said 'the future depends on what we do in the present.' There are countless people in my life that helped me along the way. I feel it's important to give back to the community."

Norris thinks being a good person is the beginning of being responsible.

"And I feel each of us is responsible to make our community a better place to live and raise our families," Norris said. "If we don't do it, who will?"

kthompson@zanesvilletimes recorder.com; (740) 450-6753

---

we are one big family and no one is better than anyone else. That had a profound impact on me. I knew that, no matter what the circumstances of our kids, by the Grace of God go I. After that experience, I would always strive to humble myself knowing we are all part of this community, and how we treat the least in our community, defines our character.

The next Director, Gerald Brandt, took the helm in 1992. Always a consummate professional, Mr. Brandt, bolstered the therapeutic services at Avondale. Simply feeling good about what we do was no longer good enough. He used statistics, data, and the latest research to support the changing program. Gerry's approach has propelled us to reach higher, loftier goals.

In her position as Indirect Service Coordinator, Janet Harper has been the cog that has kept the wheels of Avondale turning smoothly. She has been an asset to the Avondale Youth Center for thirty-three years. During her tenure, Janet has worn many "hats". In addition to her assigned duties, Janet has been the "unofficial": nurse, seamstress, cook, mother, disciplinarian, decorator, event planner, and counselor. Her vast knowledge of all things Avondale, has led us to name her the "Avondale Historian." Avondale is a "home" thanks to Janet and her service to the children and families of Muskingum County has been exemplary.

In closing, I would like to thank the current and former staff, for your hard work and dedication to the Avondale mission. Each of you has been an integral part in the continuing success of the Avondale Youth Center. Thank you for taking this wonderful journey with me.

– by Nathaniel Norris, Director 2008-Present

Opposite Page
Newspaper article from the *Zanesville Times Recorder*, titled: "Men Who Make A Difference."

153

CHAPTER 5

The Cemetery

For many years visitors have come to Avondale, and are shocked to discover that a small cemetery exists on the grounds. Almost everyone who is able, makes a visit to the five graves resting along the tree line. All of these visitors have shared the same question. How did these children die? It's not clear when the answer to this question was forgotten, or lost. Perhaps, the details were kept quiet to spare feelings or rest the fears of children living at the home. It is more likely that details just faded over time as so often happens with the distant past. Rumors have existed, and primarily passed down from the youth in the form of legend or ghost stories. It's been said that Jack Fisher fell down the steps inside the building, or that he fell from a swing outside. Some even say he haunts the back hall of the boys wing or can be heard playing with toys upstairs. It has also been printed that all the children died from an influenza epidemic. The answers were found with a little help, a lot of microfilm and even more patience.

There have been at least four deaths at The Avondale Children's Home. All four of those children are buried in the little known cemetery at the back of the west corner of the grounds. Superintendent and Matron Billingsley started the cemetery after the tragic death of Bertha Davis in 1912 just under a year after the home opened. It is documented that in September of 1920, 4 year old Bertha Davis ate several grains of concentrated lye which she thought was candy. The lye caused burns in her mouth, throat and stomach which led to her death on November 18, 1920. She was buried just two days later. Bertha's father lived in Zanesville but was unable to be found. The Billingsley's decided to bury her on

Opposite Page
Little-known cemetery located on the grounds of the Avondale Youth Center.

the grounds under a shade tree, and a local tombstone dealer donated a stone for Bertha.

Just four years later the second child to pass away at the home was two year-old Mary Lucile Grist. The cause of death listed is Measles and Exhaustion.

Ruth May Rogers, age 6 died of Influenza and Pneumonia on December 2nd, 1918 during the influenza epidemic, and was buried on December 3rd.

The last child to be buried at the Children's Home for over 60 years was Jack Fisher. The August 8th, 1930 edition of The Zanesville Signal article was titled, "Boy at Avondale Dies of Injuries-Fall From Swing Causes Fatal Hurts to Boy". The article explains that a head injury received in a fall from a swing at the Children's Home that Monday caused the death of 5 year old Jack. He was treated by a physician for the injury, and his skull was not fractured. However, late Wednesday evening Jack took a turn for the worse and was admitted to the hospital. He passed away at 3:30 a.m. on Thursday. The funeral was held Saturday 9am at the Children's Home.

Below
The only mention in Ruth's case file of her death, the third child to pass away while a resident at Avondale.

AFFIDAVIT

AS TO DEPENDENT, NEGLECTED, OR DELINQUENT CHILD

O. L. Vol. 99, Juvenile Law, Sec. 7.

THE STATE OF OHIO, } ss: **PROBATE COURT**
MUSKINGUM COUNTY.

Before me, *Harvey C. Smith* Judge and Ex-Officio Clerk of the Probate Court in Juvenile Jurisdiction in and for said County, personally came *Bertha Rogers* who, being duly sworn according to law, deposes and says, that *she* has knowledge of *Ruth May Rogers* a minor under the age of ~~seventeen~~ *eighteen* years, to-wit, about the age of *5* years, that said minor appears to be a *dependent & neglected* child in this; that her *father is dead and her mother can not properly provide for her*

Said minor is not an inmate of a state institution, or any institution incorporated under the laws of the State for the care and correction of delinquent, neglected and dependent children.

The name of the person having custody or control of said minor, or with whom the same now is, is *Bertha Rogers* and resides at *Zanesville O*

That *Bertha Rogers* the *mother* of said child resides at ³

Bertha **her** **✗** *Rogers* **mark**

and further affiant saith not.

Sworn to before me and signed in my presence, this *14* day of *May* A. D. 191*7*.

Harvey C. Smith
Probate Judge and Ex-Officio Clerk in Juvenile Jurisdiction.

            Deputy Clerk.

¹ Dependent, and¹ ted or delinquent.
² Parent, guardi n or relative, give relationship.
³ Here give place of residence, also nationality and occupation of parent or nearest relative, living or dead.

Above
The gravestone for Ruth May Rogers.

Left
The court papers which placed Ruth May Rogers at Avondale where she would pass away from influenza less than two years later.

Above
The donated gravestone for Bertha Davis.

Right
Newspaper clipping, date unknown.

LITTLE CHILD DIES FROM EATING LYE

Burns in the mouth, throat and stomach from eating concentrated lye in September caused the death of Bertha Davis, aged four years, at the Bethesda hospital Tuesday afternoon at 1 o'clock.

The child was a member of the colony of little tots at the Avondale children's home. She found some grains of lye and ate them, thinking they were candy. The results of the burns caused her death. She was taken to the hospital several days ago.

The father of the child resides in this city. He did not know of her serious illness, and the officers searched for him Tuesday night to notify him of her death. The body was prepared for burial at the People's Undertaking rooms, and is being held there until final arrangements are completed.

Right
The donated gravestone for Sharell Powell, "Baby S."

158

There were no more burials at the Avondale cemetery until 1993. On December 3rd, 1992 the *Zanesville Times Reporter* did a story on the search for a burial site for "Baby S" the county's first foster child with AIDS. The child was born to parents who both had AIDS, and the young child was dying. When diagnosed she was given six months to live, but lived almost to age 3 in misery. Sadly, the family had fled the area and there was no one willing to take responsibility for the burial. The newspaper articles pulled at the heartstrings of the community and donations began to flow. People began offering burial space in their family plots. A fund was set up and excess donations were to go to the Adopt-A-Child for Christmas and Avondale Christmas funds.

In 1996 a teddy bear monument was donated to watch over those youth in the small cemetery that sits alone behind Avondale. Thank you to those over the years who have helped maintain the grounds, left behind a flower or taken a moment to say a few words at the final resting place of these 5 young children.

Above
The gravestone for Mary Lucile Crist.

Below
The cemetery in 2011.

Above
The gravestone for Jack Fisher.

Right
There has been much rumor and speculation over the death of Jack Fisher.

Opposite Page
Document from the case file placing Jack Fisher and his siblings at Avondale.

Boy at Avondale Dies of Injuries

Fall From Swing Causes Fatal Hurts to Boy

A head injury received in a fall from a swing at the Avondale Children's home on Roseville road Monday proved fatal to Jack Marshal Fisher, five-year-old son of Edwin Fisher of 423 Putnam avenue, in Bethesda hospital at 2:30 a. m. Thursday.

The boy was treated by a physician for the injury. His skull was not fractured, the doctor said. He took a sudden turn for the worse late Wednesday night and was admitted to the hospital.

Surviving are his father of Putnam avenue, five brothers: Glenwood of Brookover avenue; Edwin, Carlisle and William at the Putnam avenue home and Dean, of the children's home; three sisters, Mrs. Roy Gebhart, Putnam avenue; Catherine of the home and Geneva of the children's home. His mother died two years ago.

Funeral services will be held at 9 o'clock Saturday morning at the Avondale children's home. Rev. James H. Kinney, of Trinity M. E. church, will be in charge. Interment will be made in a specially designated burial plot near the children's home. Mader-Peoples in charge.

Form 36—Prescribed by Division of Charities

JOURNAL ENTRY

FINDING, JUDGMENT AND ORDER OF THE COURT

General Code, Secs. 1352-3, 1352-8, 1642, 1643, 1652, 1653, 1672 and 3093

Note: A copy of this Journal Entry and a family history sheet must accompany each child

JUVENILE COURT _____Muskingum_____ COUNTY, OHIO

In the Matter of   Juvenile No._____

Dean, Geneva, Jack and Gene Fisher _____ COMMITMENT FOR (2)TEMPORARY ~~PERMANENT~~ CARE

as (1) Dependent Children SEX

This __9th__ day of __July__ 192_9_ Dean, Geneva, Jack, and Gene Fisher, ~~was~~ were

(Name of Child)

brought before the court, complained of by __Edwin L. Fisher__ with

(Name of Party Making Complaint)

being Dependent ~~Delinquent~~ a en child and the court having instituted an investigation, and having heard all the evidence finds:

That the law has been duly complied with in this case; that proper citations have been issued and due return made thereof;

That the said child was born on or about the_____day of _____19___, in the

City of __see statement for this information__, County of_____ State of_____

That the name, residence, nationality, and occupation of each parent is as follows:

Father __Edwin L. Fisher - 1020 Fernando St.,Zanesville, Ohio__

__American - painter__

Mother __Alta May Smith Fisher - deceased - American__

(Given Maiden Name)

That said children are dependent in this, that __their Mother is dead and their Father is unable to give them proper parental care.__

and therefore comes into the jurisdiction of this court, being in all respects within the provisions of the law concerning dependent and delinquent children.

The court, finding further that it is for the best interests of said child that his (3) __Father__

be deprived of its care and custody ~~temporarily~~ for the reason that (4) __he is unable to work away from home and care for said children properly.__

161

By RALPH CONLEY

One of the smallest private cemeteries in the Zanesville area, and one not generally known to the public is located at the Muskingum County Children's home.

The tiny cemetery is on a fenced plot 30 feet long and 20 feet wide, and contains four graves of children who were wards of the home at the time of their death.

Mr. and Mrs. J. B. Billingsley, who were in charge of the home from 1911 to 1935 said the cemetery began in 1912 when little Bertha Davis died November 19, 1912, as a result of accident injuries.

The child had no kown relatives and the Billingsleys decided to bury her on the home property. They chose a shaded spot near the west pasture.

After she was buried, a Zanesville tombstone dealer offered to donate stones for the cemetery. Accordingly, he erected a stone for the Davis girl.

No more burials were made in the cemetery until April 11, 1916, when an infant, Mary Lucille Crist, died at the home. She was buried beside the Davis girl. A similar stone was erected by the tombstone dealer.

Ruth May Rogers, 6, died from influenza during the epidemic in 1918, and she too was bruied in the cemetery and a stone was erected.

The last child buried in the littel plot was Jack Fisher, 4, who was fatally injured when he fell from a swing.

Jack Caughey, present superintendent of the home, is keeping the cemetery clean. Two wards of the home, Mary Axline and Lucille Lampros, do most of the mowing and grass cutting.

Caughey said a new fence is badly needed around the little cemetery. The present fence was built in 1912 after the first burial was made, and Caughey hopes to obtain a new chain fence with concrete posts.

Probably no more burials will be made there since the county now provides for burial of children who have no relatives.

But Caughey says that as long as he is superintendent of the home, the tiny cemetery will be properly maintained.

CHILDREN'S HOME MAINTAINS TINY CEMETERY
. . . Lucille Lampros and Mary Axline cut the grass.

★ ★ ★

Children's Home Keeps Up Little Known Cemetery

Above & Right
Newspaper clipping, August 5, 1951.

Opposite Page
A monument donated by Mudgett's Monuments, in 2000, to watch over these precious children.

CHAPTER 6

Epilogue
A Century of Caring
1911 ~ 2011

❖

I t was quite acceptable and prudent public policy for most all county child welfare agencies in the State of Ohio to administer, fund, and license their own residential group home for the purpose of protecting and rehabilitating needy children. However, in the past 40 years the aggregate number of county child welfare agencies in the State of Ohio who actually license and administer their own residential group home at the time of this printing (fall of 2011) stands at four. Muskingum County Children Services has, as a result of much deliberation and determination, decided that it is professionally imperative that we administer our very own child residential treatment center (Avondale Youth Center) in order that as a community of concerned caregivers we provide exceptional treatment services at the local level. Most all county child welfare agencies have slowly yet deliberately abandoned this public policy practice and purged themselves entirely of residential living business. Following are several reasons regularly cited by local child welfare officials from around the State of Ohio for abandoning the business of operating a child residential treatment center:

Residential treatment is an unfunded activity at the state and local levels of government.

The existence of enormous professional and legal liability issues.

Extremely cumbersome, invasive licensing bureaucracy.

Astronomical costs associated with operating a child residential treatment center.

Left
The meditation fountain was added in 2010 to give children and families a place of calm and relaxation.

"It was a wonderful place to work and grow as a person!"
Jill Bailey – 1979-90
(the first CCWIII who later became a supervisor at Licking County Children Services)

Above
Children bounce at the Avondale
Reunion, May 15, 2011.

Outdated and, oftentimes, illogical and ill-conceived auditing mandates (programmatic and fiscal).

Massive de-emphasis statewide in the practice of offering group living care in all social service disciplines (including child welfare, juvenile justice, education, mental health, drug & alcohol interdiction, and developmental disabilities).

Much painstaking work has been undertaken to gather together a wide range of personal recollections and anecdotes, newspaper and other media accounts, and governmental documents; all for the noble purpose of documenting the rich history of our beloved Avondale Youth Center. After this exhaustive fact-finding and research, it is truly inconceivable to imagine our Muskingum County community without an Avondale Youth Center. This program, this home built on the foundation of love and compassion, has touched and literally saved so many lives that its community impact cannot be effectively calculated.

Certainly, exceptional child welfare practice in Muskingum County is directly linked to the fortunes of the Avondale Youth Center. Who could have ever predicted or even imagined that this facility, built of brick and mortar, and this program would continue to serve it's very special population of children and families after 100 years. That is a legacy of success certainly worth celebrating and a program worth enhancing as we proceed into and throughout the 21st century.

Great books are, indeed, written to accomplish a multitude of various goals. Some books are inked to inspire, other's written to instruct, some chronicle history to create a legacy or to facilitate a call to action; It is our fervent hope that this book has accomplished all of the aforementioned.

Our solemn pledge to this wonderful Muskingum County community and to the outstanding legacy of the Avondale Youth Center is that we will continue to serve the absolute best interests of children in the least restrictive environment possible to ensure that world class child protective services are always provided on a case by case basis.

The Story Continues…

What started out as an orphanage in 1911 has transformed into a therapeutic treatment center in the modern era. In the early days, most children were at Avondale for few different reasons. The parents were either deceased or couldn't provide for their children any longer. Most of the time, living at Avondale meant a stay till adulthood. Life at the home was focused on discipline, religious faith, hard work and values instilled by the matrons. The school was on-grounds and transportation was a luxury meaning there must have been some sense of isolation from the rest of the community. Many rules and practices were upheld for decades without change. Siblings of the opposite sex only saw each other at mealtimes and were not allowed to speak. The great depression era in which over 100 youth lived in the facility surely led to discipline and control being paramount. Even in the 1960's, when the working-farm age had long passed, the operation of the home remained much the same.

The first major shift in operations of the home didn't come until 1971. Avondale became less about control, and more about concern. For the first time, the youth could speak during dinner. Siblings and other youth of the opposite sex were given opportunities to interact and spend time together. The new director, Roger Russell focused the emphasis to providing enriching experiences. Mr. Russell reintroduced horses to Avondale through donations. He made sure that any child that wanted one could be responsible for their own horse. There were also dogs, goats and other farm animals on the grounds purely for the purpose of creating a better environment for those who never had such opportunities. Mr. Russell gathered donated golf balls and clubs and built a makeshift golf course on the front lawn. Avondale became less of an institution and more like a very large loving and caring foster home.

By the late 1970's, Avondale would again change to suit the needs of the community. The kids being placed at Avondale were becoming more difficult. Social problems of the time were beginning to become more extreme and as a result, Avondale started to see more youth with mental health and drug & alcohol issues. For the first time, a therapeutic treatment program was implemented by the new Director Charlie Jones. The Avondale Children's Home would begin to be called the Avondale Youth Center. In the beginning, Avondale would take youth from nearly birth on up. By the

Above
Gary King, Public Information Officer and Human Resources Officer for Muskingum County Children Services, 2008-present. Gary also worked at the Avondale Youth Center as a Child Care Worker and Team Leader from 1996 to 2005.

"I loved it here and really liked going places with Bill Loader; he was so fun. Laurie Cunningham did miracles for me. Laurie took me and others to Magic Mountain!"

Haleigh Caplinger – 2000-01

Right
Christmas at Avondale, 2009.

time of the Caugheys, residents needed to be at least of school age. During the late 1970s, licensing mandated that residents must be at least 12 years of age.

Upon his arrival at Avondale, Director Charlie Jones already had a strong background in counseling youth and working with mental health issues. Mr. Jones introduced a behavior modification treatment program which would raise the professionalism and forever change the Avondale approach to kids. By the 1980's the 'point system' had become integral. Mr. Jones valued the importance of having quality well-trained staff. Having a more structured program meant that not just anyone could work with the kids. It took special people who shared a commitment to helping kids improve their lives. There was a growing number of experienced staff who were skilled at working with youth, but also provided a caring atmosphere in which kids could heal and find their way in life. The sense of home and family was there for those who needed it, but also structure. Youth were not staying at the center as long as they had decades before, but they were still averaging several years. The stay for most kids was still long enough that it would become 'home'. Mr. Jones and staff bridged a gap between 'family atmosphere' and treatment.

By the mid 1990's, under the direction of Gerry Brandt, a shift occurred in the child welfare system that would again change Avondale. There was a movement towards, 'Family-Centered Practice'. Rather than simply focusing therapy on the child, this new approach would incorporate the entire family. The hope is not only to stabilize the child, but also the family and strengthen their relationships. This new approach led to much shorter average stays of 4-6 months. Mr. Brandt believed in placing more responsibility on those who knew the children best. Therefore, Child Care Workers began writing Service Plans and taking direct responsibility for specific youth through a Sponsorship Program. Although this is a more refined intensive approach to treatment, it has affected how residents feel about Avondale. Most of today's kids no longer view the facility as home, but more as a temporary stay until they can get into a permanent living situation. There is some level of hope that no child will get too 'settled' staying there, and instead be focused on working toward a placement in another home. This change in how youth perceive the home was intentional and, in truth, has probably taken place over decades. Even in the earliest days certainly there were those that viewed Avondale as home and others that never saw it quite that way.

The new millennium would bring the next transition to the Avondale program. The point system which had worked well for many years had become a bit restrictive. Since, youth were now expected to stay a much shorter period of time, the process of advancement from Zone 1 to Zone 5 became too difficult and didn't fit as well within the family-centered approach that was now firmly in place.

A new goal-focused program was developed. Put simply, each youth who enters Avondale is responsible for designing their own program within certain parameters. Their status in the program is based on achievement of goals, which they create, and directly

Above
David Boyer, Executive Director of Muskingum County Children Services, portrays "Old Saint Nick" at the 2010 Avondale Youth Center Old Fashioned Christmas Celebration. The girl in the picture is Morgan Cooper.

Above
The beginning of our search for former residents from the early days. Director, Nate Norris and Executive Director, Dave Boyer welcome Eileen Dennis back to her childhood home.

Right
Linda and Roger Russell sharing memories with Nate Norris on the Avondale back lawn.

Opposite Page
Roger Russell and former resident Rose Oliver reunited for the first time in many years.

relates to what needs to happen to be placed outside of Avondale. This system empowers youth by making them accountable for their own success and challenges. The goal-system also serves to better meet the individual needs of each child in the program. This program is currently still in place, however as time goes on surely the 'needs' will change and Avondale will once again adapt to follow suit.

The current Director, Nate Norris, has built upon Avondale's strong foundation. Mr. Norris has increased the intensity of treatment by integrating more mental health services such as an on-site therapist and in-house psychiatric visits and psychologist consultations. Mental health providers such as Six County, Inc., and Thompkins Center have continued long-standing relationships.

In the past several years, visitors may also notice tremendous upgrades and remodelling to the building. Great effort is put into keeping Avondale as a comfortable and quality home for children.

Avondale Leadership

James and Velma Billingsley, Superintendent and Matron
1911-1934

J. Fred Lane and Louise Gibson, Superintendent and Matron
1935-1945

Jesse and Blanche Hutson, Superintendent and Matron
1945-1949

John (Jack) S. and Sarah A. Caughey, Superintendent and Matron
1949-1964

Sarah Caughey, Superintendent
1964-1971

Roger & Linda Russell, Director and Matron
1971- 1974

William Dawson, Director
1974-1975

Richard Evilsizer, Director
1976-1977

Mildred Way, Interim Director
May 1977-June 1977

Charlie Jones, Director
1977-1991

Claudia Hammack, Interim Director
1991

Gerry Brandt, Director
1991-2008

Nathaniel Norris, Director
2008-Present

Avondale Timeline

July 1909 – Avondale land was purchased for $7572

March 6th, 1911 – J.B. Billingsley appointed Superintendent of Avondale Children's Home and his wife Velma was appointed Matron

November 12, 1911- Avondale Children's Home Opened (42 Children Placed)

November 19, 1912 – 4 year Bertha Davis died at Avondale, and The Muskingum Children's Cemetery was created.

September 1916 – Trustees Authorized the first automobile for the home and purchase of a "Chevrolet Machine" was made from Buckeye Motor Co. for $560.70.

November/December 1918 – Children were removed because of an Influenza epidemic

1924 – The Avondale Children's Home School Opened

December 1924 – 75 residents

Thanksgiving 1925 – 45 residents

February 1930 – Over 100 residents

March 1931 – 144 residents

December 1934 – James and Velma Billingsley resigned as Superintendent and Matron.

March 1st, 1935 – J. Fred Lane Superintendent, and Marjorie Gibson as Matron

December 1939 – 72 residents

1945 – Jesse Hutson (Blanche Hutson-Wife) Appointed Superintendent

1946 – Muskingum County Child Welfare Board formed

1949 – Mr. and Mrs. Jesse Hutson Superintendents-Resigned

August 17, 1949 – John S. Caughey and Sara A. Caughey appointed Superintendent and Matron.

March 1958 – 50 residents

February 22, 1964 – John (Jack) S. Caughey died

March 1, 1964 – Sarah Caughey Acting Director ($300 per Month)

September 1, 1971 – Roger Russell, Director

1973 – Barn Burnt Down

July 1974 – Bill Dawson, Director

January 1975 – Bill Dawson Resigned

June 7, 1976 – Richard Evilsizer, Director

June 24, 1977 – Richard Evilsizer Resigned

June 1977 – Mildred Way Interim Director

October 10, 1977 – Charlie Jones, Director

June 1978 – 24 residents

May 1979 – Bill Anderson hired as Executive Director Muskingum County Children Services.

November 30, 1991 – Charlie Jones Retired/ Gerry Brandt, Director

March 31, 2008 – Gerry Brandt-Retired

April 2008 – Nate Norris, Director

November 2011 – 22 residents

November 23, 2011 – 100 years of Children living at the home.